LARRY COHEN'S

BIDDING CHALLENGE

D1399472

MASTER POINT PRESS • TORONTO

Master Point Press
331 Douglas Ave.
Toronto, Ontario Canada
M5M 1H2
(416) 781-0351 Fax (416) 781-1831
Internet www.masterpointpress.com

Canadian Cataloguing in Publication Data
Cohen, Larry, 1959-
Larry Cohen's Bidding challenge

ISBN 1-894154-45-2

1. Contract bridge — Bidding I. Title
GV1282.435.C63 2002   795.41'52 C2001-904149-7

Editor	Ray Lee
Cover and Interior design	Olena S. Sullivan
Interior format and copyediting	Deanna Bourassa

Printed and bound in Canada by Webcom Ltd.

1 2 3 4 5 6 7   06 05 04 03 02

Contents

Acknowledgements

The material in this book is based on articles that originally appeared in *Bridge Today* magazine and is reprinted here by permission.

Photo Credits

Ray Lee: 13, 35, 47, 69, 91, 113

Ron Tacchi: 47

HOW TO USE THIS BOOK

This book presents you with a unique opportunity to match your bidding skills against the world's best. Each of the seven chapters in this book contains a set of challenging bidding problems from an Invitational Pairs event that involved some of the world's top players. Before reading a chapter, turn to the back of the book, where you will find the hands for each problem. The pages are perforated so that if you wish, you can tear them out of the book. There are two copies of each set of hands, so even after you take out one set, the book will still have a copy of all the hands. Try bidding them with your favorite partner, and make a note of the final contract that you reach. Now you are ready to compare your results against a group of world-class pairs on the same hands.

Top international pairs events are usually scored using IMPs, in the following manner. The best and worst score on each deal is thrown out, so if there are eight tables in play, six scores remain. The 'datum' against which you score is the average of those six remaining scores, rounded off. Suppose the datum on a certain board was calculated as +1110. That would mean that if you and your partner, or any competitors in the event, bid and made 6NT on this board for plus 1440, you would win 330 points and score 8 IMPs. For making 6♣ you'd win 260 points and gain 7 IMPs. The datum scores given for each deal in this book are exactly the ones that were achieved in real life. For scoring purposes, you will always be the same direction for an entire chapter (either East–West or North–South), and the datum score will be relative to your direction. If the datum is +1110, as in our previous example, then that is the score in your direction with which you must compare your own result. If the contract you arrive at is not among those I discuss, try to estimate the likely result and work out your own IMP score against the datum given. For scoring convenience, all the datums and vulnerabilities are listed on the last page of each chapter. You can also use the IMP table on page 158.

In general, if you get to the correct contract you will be rewarded. The kind of deal where you can overbid to a lucky slam that happens to make — or reach an unlucky one that should be bid but goes down — is not part of this book. Of course, you can simply read through the book as an account of some interesting deals from top-level tournaments. However, you'll gain more insight into the issues and difficulties on each pair of hands if you try them yourself first. You'll also undoubtedly discover areas of bidding that you need to discuss with your partner.

My partner in each of these events was David Berkowitz. I will tell you what happened at my table on these hands (and trust me, it will be embarrassing at times), and give some of the other results as well, along with a sprinkling of my opinions. Perhaps you will be less interested in my advice though, when you see the results David and I achieved. No laughing permitted.

In summary, then, you can approach this book one of two ways. You can simply read it, as an account of 140 interesting deals played in top-level competition over the past few years. However, I think you'll get much more out of it if you bid the hands yourself first, and then read the commentary. Stack your score up against the experts — you may do better, and in many cases, you can hardly do worse!

INTRODUCTION
BY ANDREW ROBSON

The Cap Gemini has become known universally among the cognoscenti as the Wimbledon — or the Masters in golf parlance — of bridge. You are treated as the best in the world, and the pomp of the occasion gives the bridge an added zest.

The 2000 Cap Gemini was especially exciting for me. Playing with Zia — a previous four-time winner and universally adored, being one of too few experts who give back to the game some of what they gain from it — ensured that we had a massive following wind. After a less than inspiring start that saw us in eighth place out of 16 after nine of the 15 matches, we launched a charge, but only overtook the long-time leaders (Steve Weinstein and Bobby Levin) on the final two hands. In tournaments such as this, where all the competitors are first-class, it is often the most subtle nuance that makes one result different from another. On these two hands, the auctions at our table and at that of the leaders were similar, but not precisely the same.

On the first (Board 29) we bid a vulnerable game missed by the entire field. With one opponent holding a strong notrump this was hardly surprising. In truth the auction 'tempoed' well for us:

Board 29

Both Vul.
Dealer South

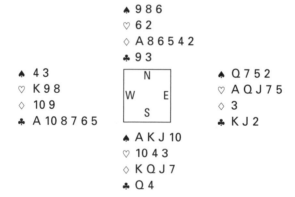

♠ 986
♡ 6 2
◇ A 8 6 5 4 2
♣ 9 3

♠ 4 3
♡ K 9 8
◇ 10 9
♣ A 10 8 7 6 5

N
W E
S

♠ Q 7 5 2
♡ A Q J 7 5
◇ 3
♣ K J 2

♠ A K J 10
♡ 10 4 3
◇ K Q J 7
♣ Q 4

Leaders' Table

MIHOV	WEINSTEIN	NANEV	LEVIN
SOUTH	WEST	NORTH	EAST
1NT	pass	2NT	dbl
3◇	4♣	(all pass)	

Our Table

NAB	ZIA	BERTENS	ROBSON
SOUTH	WEST	NORTH	EAST
1NT	pass	2NT	pass
3♣	dbl	3◇	dbl
pass	3♡	pass	4♡
(all pass)			

At both tables the auction began with a 1NT opening and a conventional 2NT response, showing a diamond suit (with strength yet to be revealed). At the leaders' table, Levin's double of 2NT was for takeout, and over South's rebid of 3◇, Weinstein (West) bid 4♣. This scored 130 for a gain of 5 IMPs to the leaders. At our table, we managed to reach the heart game.

Really, we were fortunate that our opponent gave us the opportunity. My style is not to get involved with an immediate double of a transfer, but to wait until the auction dies on the next round. As I was waiting to see what would happen, Zia entered the auction ahead of me. He doubled a transfer break (South's 3♣ was artificial, showing support for diamonds). Zia's double showed clubs and my double of 3◇ was responsive, as they had 'bid and raised' diamonds. Zia replied in his three-card suit and I raised to the thin game. The main difference in the two auctions was South's second bid. At our table, the 3♣ bid allowed the cheap double by Zia and gave us more room to find hearts. Plus 620 certainly felt good and we won 12 IMPs on the hand.

On the very last hand (Board 30) of the event, both North–South pairs reached a normal but pushy major-suit game in a 5-3 fit.

Board 30

Neither Vul.
Dealer West

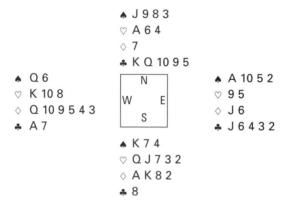

```
                    ♠ J 9 8 3
                    ♡ A 6 4
                    ◊ 7
                    ♣ K Q 10 9 5
  ♠ Q 6                             ♠ A 10 5 2
  ♡ K 10 8          ┌─── N ───┐     ♡ 9 5
  ◊ Q 10 9 5 4 3    W       E        ◊ J 6
  ♣ A 7             └─── S ───┘     ♣ J 6 4 3 2
                    ♠ K 7 4
                    ♡ Q J 7 3 2
                    ◊ A K 8 2
                    ♣ 8
```

Leaders' Table

MIHOV	WEINSTEIN	NANEV	LEVIN
SOUTH	WEST	NORTH	EAST
	1◊	dbl	pass
2◊	pass	2♠	pass
3♡	pass	4♡	(all pass)

Our Table

NAB	ZIA	BERTENS	ROBSON
SOUTH	WEST	NORTH	EAST
	2◊	pass	3◊
3♡	pass	4♡	(all pass)

At the leaders' table, Weinstein led the ♣A and Levin signaled with the 6. Weinstein switched to the ♠Q. This was a reasonable try, hoping to find partner with the ♠K and ♡J to defeat the contract. After this start, there was nothing the defenders could do. Levin (East) overtook with his ace to lead back a club, in case his partner had led a singleton ace. Declarer was now able to take the marked finesse in hearts and lose only three tricks to score his contract.

At our table, Zia started the auction with a weak two-bid, apparently an American, or New York, variation (on the heavy side). This start hid the fact that he held most of the high cards and helped a great deal to fool declarer. The opponents reached game and Zia also chose to attack with the ♣A from ♣A-x. In a (misguided) effort to ensure partner's switch to a spade, I dropped the jack from J6432. It was extravagant and, thank goodness, Zia ignored me, playing his second club to dummy's 9. Now remember the weak two-bid. Declarer thought the ♡K was more likely to be in my hand than Zia's, so he made a technically sound play of a low heart from dummy. If I won the ♡K, he could ruff a club return high and still draw trumps. But the play backfired. On the lead of a heart to the jack, it was Zia who won the king. He next put me in with my ♠A to lead a third club. A second trump trick was promoted, the contract failed, and the event was ours. *Phew!*

It would be nice for me to say (for the sake of this book) that I put our victory down to the bidding of practice hands. It was not so — I arrived a quarter of an hour before the start of the tournament and we both forgot to bring any practice hands. Nevertheless, bidding practice hands and discussing the inferences and so forth is probably the best way to improve a keen partnership's results. Note that Zia and I did not perform well until the last third of the tournament, when we had 150 deals under our belts.

I would like to recommend this book to all players, because it is more than just a bidding practice. In allowing you to compare your results against the auctions in real life, Larry Cohen gives you something to aspire to. Maybe one day you, too, will get a chance to compete in the world's most lavish tournament.

Andrew Robson,
London, England

CAP VOLMAC 1995

The 1995 Cap Volmac winners were Zia Mahmood and Michael Rosenberg, but, as always, the real winner of this event was the game of bridge. This year there were an unusually high number of constructive bidding decisions. By focusing on twenty such deals, a lot can be learned about bidding. While it might be depressing for the sixteen pairs of participants, it should give hope to everyone else out there! As you'll see, the masters were far from masterful. Have you and your favorite partnership tried to test yourselves (pages 159 and 167)? Perhaps you can outbid the best players in the world!

ZIA MAHMOOD

MICHAEL ROSENBERG

DEAL 1

Dealer South, E-W Vul.
E-W Datum +1110

*South passes and later
enters with a diamond
bid at any level.*

```
              ♠ A 6 2
              ♡ 10 8 7 5 3      .
              ◇ Q 4 3
              ♣ 6 5
 ♠ K J 8 7    ┌─────────┐    ♠ Q
 ♡ A Q 4      │    N    │    ♡ K J 6
 ◇ A 10 6     │ W     E │    ◇ 7
 ♣ Q 10 3     │    S    │    ♣ A K J 9 8 7 4 2
              └─────────┘
              ♠ 10 9 5 4 3
              ♡ 9 2
              ◇ K J 9 8 5 2
              ♣ —
```

You might expect an expert field to reach the small slam, but South's interference caused several pairs some difficulty. At one table, Dutch stars Westra and Leufkens never interfered with the North-South cards. This gave their countrymen, Maas-Kirchoff, a free run. West opened 1NT and East eventually used Gerber to reach 6NT for 1440. Three South players, Ofir Herbst of Israel, Gabriel Chagas of Brazil, and Tony Forrester of Great Britain, opened the South hand with a diamond preempt. However, this was brushed aside with a notrump overcall, an ace-ask and a successful small slam for Indonesia's Lasut-Manoppo, Norway's Helgemo-Helness, and Poland's Lesniewski-Szymanowski.

France's Levy-Mouiel and Denmark's Auken-Koch also reached a small slam when West started with 1NT. East showed clubs, and South interfered on the three-level. Again East was able to Blackwood on the next round. Both pairs knew that the delayed jump to 4NT was not quantitative.

The two pairs that got this one wrong were a new partnership and a 20-year partnership. The late Edgar Kaplan and Bobby Wolff started 1NT-4♣, Gerber. After South's 4◇, confusion ensued and eventually 7♣ doubled was reached, minus 200. At the eighth table, Jeff Meckstroth opened 1NT and Eric Rodwell responded 4♣. South bid 4◇, and again there was a mix-up. I'm sure Jeff and Eric have discussed interference over Gerber, but even the world's best have their lapses. They ended up in 7NT doubled down one.

It is a bit unfair that six North-South pairs had to lose 8 IMPs for being in the wrong place at the wrong time, but perhaps they should have preempted a bit more aggressively.

Score yourself as follows : 7NT or 7♣ — 16 IMPs; 6NT +8 IMPs; 6♣ +7 IMPs; any game contract — 10 IMPs

Dealer West, Both Vul.
E–W Datum +670

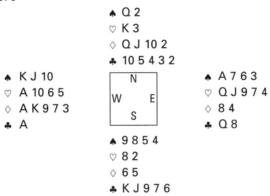

```
                    ♠ Q 2
                    ♡ K 3
                    ◊ Q J 10 2
                    ♣ 10 5 4 3 2
   ♠ K J 10                              ♠ A 7 6 3
   ♡ A 10 6 5         N                  ♡ Q J 9 7 4
   ◊ A K 9 7 3    W       E              ◊ 8 4
   ♣ A                 S                 ♣ Q 8
                    ♠ 9 8 5 4
                    ♡ 8 2
                    ◊ 6 5
                    ♣ K J 9 7 6
```

This deal was a test in both the bidding and the play. Again, only six of the eight pairs hit the target in the bidding. Six hearts is clearly where you want to be. It's "cold" if the heart finesse wins, and has lots of other chances.   Both Forrester–Robson and Dutch world-women's-pairs champs Carla Arnolds-Bep Vriend bid 1◊-1♡, 4♣-4♡, pass. I think the East hand is too good to sign-off after West's splinter. After the same 1◊-1♡, 4♣ start, Ofir Herbst, Enri Leufkens, Gabriel Chagas, and Zia all Blackwooded into 6♡. Just for the record, Blackwood was a 4♠ bid, 'Kickback,' (as opposed to 4NT) by all four pairs.   France's Chemla-Perron reached slam via 1◊-1♡, 2♠-3♠, 4♡-5♡, 6♡, and Berkowitz and I also got to 6♡, after a Precision club start.

As you can see from the datum score, not everyone made six hearts! Two declarers received a spade lead, and scored an easy 1430. Three declarers received a club lead and went down via this simple line of play: Win the club, cross in spades for the losing heart finesse, and then hope the diamonds or spades come in. As you can see, diamonds were 4-2, and the spade was wrong. The only declarer to make the hand after a club lead was Michael Rosenberg. He played two high diamonds and ruffed a diamond with the ♡Q. He ruffed a club and ruffed another diamond high. 'Knowing' that the heart finesse was wrong, he crossed to the ♡A and exited with a heart, endplaying North, for +1430. As Michael explained later, he didn't want to put all his eggs in one basket by crossing to the ♠A at Trick 2. He figured he could always guess the ♠Q later! Nice to have such confidence, but I'm still not convinced that his line of play is better than that taken by the three declarers who failed.

The pairs that stopped in 4♡ were lucky to get a 'push' on the board, since the datum score was +670. Lots of IMPs were swung (13 either way) depending on declarer's line of play in 6♡. These IMP pair games put an extraordinary amount of weight on deals such as this. If you and your partner reached 6♡, you can take 1430 and 13 IMPs; if you didn't, you break even. Do you think I'm being too generous? Don't worry, you'll get the worst of it a few deals from now.

DEAL 3

Dealer East, N–S Vul.
E–W Datum +750

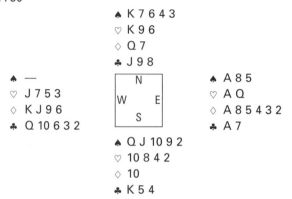

```
                    ♠ K 7 6 4 3
                    ♡ K 9 6
                    ◇ Q 7
                    ♣ J 9 8
    ♠ —                  N          ♠ A 8 5
    ♡ J 7 5 3                       ♡ A Q
    ◇ K J 9 6       W       E       ◇ A 8 5 4 3 2
    ♣ Q 10 6 3 2         S          ♣ A 7
                    ♠ Q J 10 9 2
                    ♡ 10 8 4 2
                    ◇ 10
                    ♣ K 5 4
```

It's interesting that three of the eight South players chose to make a 1♠ overcall at unfavorable vulnerability after East's 1◇ opening. Let's track the action at those three tables. Andrew Robson jumped to 4◇ with the West hand, and after North's 4♠, Tony Forrester jumped to the cold 6◇. Marcello Branco raised gently to 2◇, and North preempted to 3♠. Gabriel Chagas cuebid 4♠, and then continued on to 6◇ over West's 5◇. Berry Westra chose to make a negative double after the 1♠ overcall. He later supported diamonds, and his partner drove to 6◇. At one table, South passed, but his partner overcalled 1♠ after West's 1♡ response! East rebid 3◇ and South raised to 3♠. West, Ofir Herbst, cuebid 4♠, and his brother, Ilan, drove all the way to 7◇! With the friendly lie of the heart suit, this contract rolled home for 1440.

At a fifth table, David Berkowitz opened the East hand a Precision club, and soon reached 6◇ without any interference from Kaplan–Wolff. The other three tables missed the slam. Chemla–Perron and Arnold–Vriend bid unimpeded 1◇-1♡-2NT-3NT and scored +400 after a spade lead. At the last table, Zia chose to open the East hand with 2NT. Michael Rosenberg bid Stayman, and followed up with a natural 4♣. Zia signed off in 4NT, and had to take the heart finesse to score his 10 tricks. Because three pairs missed the slam (one of those was thrown out of the datum, along with the grand slam) the datum score was only 750, and it was worth 5 IMPs to reach 6◇. For stopping in game you lose 6 IMPs.

Dealer North, E–W Vul.
E–W Datum +1110

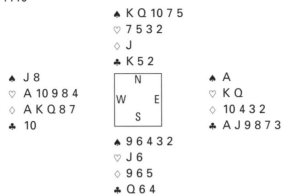

```
              ♠ K Q 10 7 5
              ♡ 7 5 3 2
              ◊ J
              ♣ K 5 2
  ♠ J 8            N          ♠ A
  ♡ A 10 9 8 4                ♡ K Q
  ◊ A K Q 8 7   W      E      ◊ 10 4 3 2
  ♣ 10              S         ♣ A J 9 8 7 3
              ♠ 9 6 4 3 2
              ♡ J 6
              ◊ 9 6 5
              ♣ Q 6 4
```

In modern times I would expect many players to preempt as the dealer at favorable vulnerability with the North hand. I realize that more conservative bidders won't like such a thought, so maybe they'll be pleased that six out of the eight Norths were able to restrain themselves. (Of course, an opening 2♠ bid wouldn't work out quite as well if we switched the South hand with either the East or West hand.)

One preemptor was Norway's star, Geir Helgemo. He opened with a Multi-2◊ and Bobby Wolff overcalled 3♣. Tor Helness bid 3♡ (pass/correct) and Edgar Kaplan chose to bid 4◊. Wolff had no cuebid available, because the opponent's suit had not been revealed! So he contented himself with a raise to 5◊, which ended the auction, plus 640. The other perpetrator was Marcello Branco, who opened the North hand 2♠. Michel Perron overcalled 3♣ and Gabriel Chagas jumped to 5♠. Paul Chemla doubled this for down four, 1100 to East-West — no swing, since the datum was 1110.

Levy-Mouiel, Berkowitz and I, and Mahmood-Rosenberg reached 6◊ after getting some spade interference from the opponents. Plus 1390 was worth 7 IMPs to each of us. Auken-Koch and Arnolds-Vriend also got spade interference, but stopped in 4♡ to lose 10 IMPs. One pair managed to reach 7◊, but this time it was a very desirable place to be. Meckstroth started with a Precision 2♣, and Lasut-Manoppo never got into the auction. Five artificial rounds of bidding later, Meckwell chalked up +2140 and 14 IMPs.

Dealer West, Neither Vul.
E–W Datum +560

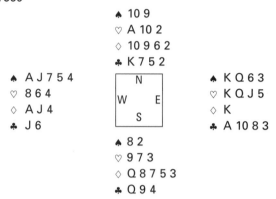

Again, we have a potential initial action that will meet with disapproval from many. This time, three of the eight West players chose to open 1♠. One of those three players would open this hand in his sleep: Jeff Meckstroth started with 1♠ but Eric Rodwell is well aware of how light his pair opens, and he eventually stopped in 4♠. The other two 1♠ openers, Enri Leufkens and Geir Helgemo, were dragged by their partners, kicking and screaming, into 6♠. Berry Westra and Tor Helness both responded with Jacoby 2NT and their partners showed a flat minimum. Blackwood followed, and then 6♠. Dennis Koch chose to under-lead his ♡A against Westra–Leufkens and was soon minus 980. David Berkowitz led a club and Geir Helgemo quickly called for dummy's eight. After a little suffering I put up the queen, and was soon rewarded with plus 50. At the other five tables West passed as dealer and four of those pairs stopped in 4♠. At the fifth table Chemla–Perron reached 6♠, making after a trump lead.

Even though the correct contract in a bidding competition is 4♠, in real life two out of the three pairs that reached a slam made it. If you and your partner stopped correctly in 4♠, you can assume you made 480, but still lose 2 IMPs. If you opened the West hand and reached a slam, you'll have to assume a club lead and minus 11 IMPs.

However, if you reached slam after West passed and East opened 1♣, you can credit yourself with +980 and win 9 IMPs, because a club lead would be unlikely.

Dealer North, E–W Vul.
E–W Datum +500

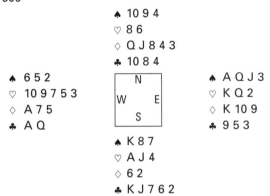

```
                    ♠ 10 9 4
                    ♡ 8 6
                    ◇ Q J 8 4 3
                    ♣ 10 8 4
  ♠ 6 5 2           ┌─────────┐        ♠ A Q J 3
  ♡ 10 9 7 5 3      │    N    │        ♡ K Q 2
  ◇ A 7 5           │ W     E │        ◇ K 10 9
  ♣ A Q            │    S    │        ♣ 9 5 3
                    └─────────┘
                    ♠ K 8 7
                    ♡ A J 4
                    ◇ 6 2
                    ♣ K J 7 6 2
```

As usual, there was a North–South pair that managed to get into the auction. It's very rare at this level of competition to see the same auction at all every table. The Dutch players are very fond of their 2♣ opening, which is used, among other things, to show a hand with 0-5 HCP and any five-card suit. Accordingly, Anton Maas opened the North hand 2♣. South responded 2◇ (perforce) and North passed to show diamonds. Carla Arnolds reopened with a double, and then raised Bep Vriend's 2♡ to 4♡, for plus 620.

At all other tables East showed a strong notrump. Four auctions started, as most of you probably did, 1NT-2◇, 2♡-3NT, leaving it up to East. While the 4-3-3-3 shape might argue for the notrump game, I think the three small clubs are reason enough to remove to 4♡. Enri Leufkens passed 3NT for minus 100, while Eric Rodwell, Michel Perron and Tor Helness opted for 4♡ and were rewarded with +620 and 3 IMPs. At another table, Edgar Kaplan began with Stayman over 1NT, showed five hearts, but then also ended in 3NT, down one. At the last two tables, Chagas-Branco and Lasut-Manoppo reached 4♡ after East opened one of a minor. If you reached 3NT, it's -12 IMPs.

DEAL 7

Dealer South, E–W Vul.
E–W Datum +360

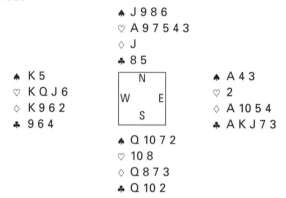

```
              ♠ J 9 8 6
              ♡ A 9 7 5 4 3
              ◇ J
              ♣ 8 5
  ♠ K 5                          ♠ A 4 3
  ♡ K Q J 6         N            ♡ 2
  ◇ K 9 6 2    W         E       ◇ A 10 5 4
  ♣ 9 6 4           S            ♣ A K J 7 3
              ♠ Q 10 7 2
              ♡ 10 8
              ◇ Q 8 7 3
              ♣ Q 10 2
```

We were in the wrong place at the wrong time, sitting N–S on this deal against Zia and Rosenberg. Michael was the only player out of eight to pass the West hand. They easily avoided the doomed slam and gained 6 IMPs against the 360 datum. Still, I think the other pairs should have avoided slam, even after the opening bid. All the other Wests, as would I, opened the West hand 1◇, and five Norths jumped preemptively to 2♡. At this point the Easts came up with four different actions! What is your choice after your partner's 1◇ is overcalled with 2♡?

Eric Rodwell, facing a Precision 1◇, chose to cuebid 3♡ and pass his partner's 3NT for plus 600 and 6 IMPs. Carla Arnolds chose 3♣ and over partner's 3NT continued with 4◇ and then passed 5◇, down one (-10 IMPs). Eddy Manoppo, also facing a Precision 1◇, chose to make a negative double of 2♡ and raised 2NT to 3NT for plus 600. Ofir Herbst and Enri Leufkens chose 4♡ over 2♡, then 6◇ over 5◇, down 200 (that's 11 away). At the other two tables the North players, Szymanowski and Levy, overcalled only 1♡. This gave Kirchoff-Maas and Auken-Koch lots of room, and after two tries by East, they duly stopped in 3NT.

Dealer West, Neither Vul.
E–W Datum +100

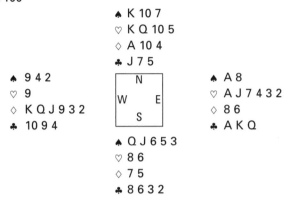

♠ K 10 7
♡ K Q 10 5
◇ A 10 4
♣ J 7 5

♠ 9 4 2
♡ 9
◇ K Q J 9 3 2
♣ 10 9 4

♠ A 8
♡ A J 7 4 3 2
◇ 8 6
♣ A K Q

♠ Q J 6 5 3
♡ 8 6
◇ 7 5
♣ 8 6 3 2

Only two of the eight pairs managed to reach the top spot of 5◇, and they both had the same auction. Lesniewski-Szymanowski and the Herbst brothers both bid 3◇-3♡, 4◇-5◇, pass, for 7 IMPs. David Berkowitz also opened 3◇, but passed my non-forcing 3♡ response, and we were minus 50 (lose 4 IMPs). The only other West preemptor was Marcello Branco, who started with 2◇. North doubled, East passed, and South bid 2♠, passed back around to Chagas. He contented himself with 3◇, ending the auction and winning 2 IMPs.

The other four Wests passed as dealer and heard four different auctions. Andrew Robson opened the North hand 1♡, and Henry Lasut tried an eccentric 1NT overcall. West, Manoppo, transferred to 3◇, ending the auction. At the other tables where West passed, North opened in clubs or notrump, East overcalled in hearts and subsequently played in 3♡ or 4♡, down 50 or 100.

DEAL 9

Dealer North, E–W Vul.
E–W Datum +1120

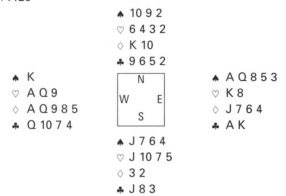

```
                      ♠ 10 9 2
                      ♡ 6 4 3 2
                      ◇ K 10
                      ♣ 9 6 5 2
   ♠ K                   N           ♠ A Q 8 5 3
   ♡ A Q 9          W         E      ♡ K 8
   ◇ A Q 9 8 5          S           ◇ J 7 6 4
   ♣ Q 10 7 4                        ♣ A K
                      ♠ J 7 6 4
                      ♡ J 10 7 5
                      ◇ 3 2
                      ♣ J 8 3
```

If you reached 7◇, would you know how to play the trump suit? Low to the
queen is slightly better than leading the jack. As you can tell, it's all moot, since
the king was offside. As you can also see from the datum score, more than one
pair reached the grand slam. To bid a grand slam on a finesse at this form of scoring is not necessarily a bad idea, but this grand was on a bit more than just a
finesse, because the ◇ 10 was also missing.

You would think this time there'd be no North–South interference. Don't
bet on it! All you have to do is look for one of the Dutch pairs and that afore-
mentioned 2♣ beast appears. In this instance Enri Leufkens opened that North
hand 2♣ (showing God knows what!), but Lesniewski-Szymanowski survived,
stopping in 6◇. Five pairs used Key Card Blackwood to stop in 6◇ and gain 6
IMPs. Chagas-Branco and Kaplan-Wolff reached 7◇, throwing 15 juicy IMPs into
the coffers of Kirchoff-Maas and Zia-Rosenberg. You've got to be on the right
side of this sort of board to have any chance of winning under this scoring system.

Dealer East, Both Vul.
E–W Datum +1460

South overcalls in hearts and North jump-raises.

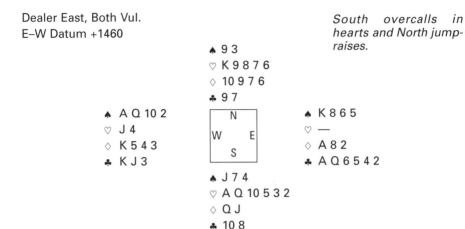

```
              ♠ 9 3
              ♡ K 9 8 7 6
              ◇ 10 9 7 6
              ♣ 9 7
♠ A Q 10 2      N        ♠ K 8 6 5
♡ J 4                    ♡ —
◇ K 5 4 3    W     E     ◇ A 8 2
♣ K J 3         S        ♣ A Q 6 5 4 2
              ♠ J 7 4
              ♡ A Q 10 5 3 2
              ◇ Q J
              ♣ 10 8
```

There was a different auction at all eight tables and three different final contracts. That datum of 1460 was achieved because there were four pairs in 6♠ (1460), two in 4♠ (710, lose 13 IMPs) and two in 7♠ (2210, win 13 IMPs). The spade grand is a very good proposition, because it can still be made against some 4-1 trump breaks. At least nobody got to 7♣, which must fail (and costs you 17 IMPs).

Four Easts started with a natural 2♣, and three of them had a free run. Kaplan-Wolff bid 2♣-2◇, 2♠-4♠, pass to lose 13 IMPs. Lasut-Manoppo bid 2♣-2◇, 2♠-4◇, 4♡-6♠, pass. I suppose 4◇ was some sort of cuebid in support of spades. Lesniewski-Szymanowski also started 2♣-2◇ but then science took over and they were soon in 7♠. I also opened 2♣, but we were opposing Meckwell, and they don't like to give their opponents a free run. Jeff bid 2♡ and after a negative double Eric raised to 3♡. (A raise to 4♡ would really have made it tougher.) After this start we managed to get only to 6♠ for a push.

The other four Easts started with 1♣, making it easy for South to get in. Helness, Mouiel, and Maas all overcalled 2♡, and after a negative double their partners raised to 5♡, 4♡, and 4♡ respectively. The openers now bid their spades, and it was up to the negative doubler. Ilan Herbst raised his brother's 5♠ to 6♠. Bep Vriend passed her partner's 4♠. Marcello Branco raised his partner's 4♠ to 5♠, and Chagas continued with 6◇, but Marcello bid only 6♠ to end the auction. At the last table, Michel Perron chose to overcall only 1♡. Jens Auken doubled and Chemla raised to 4♡. Dennis Koch chose to bid 5♡ (whereas everyone else had settled for a minimum spade bid), and his partner jumped directly to 7♠; well done.

Dealer North, Neither Vul.
E–W Datum +840

South bids hearts and
North raises.

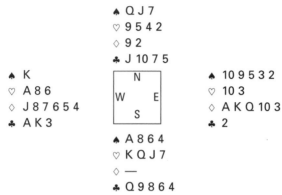

```
                    ♠ Q J 7
                    ♡ 9 5 4 2
                    ◇ 9 2
                    ♣ J 10 7 5
      ♠ K               N          ♠ 10 9 5 3 2
      ♡ A 8 6                      ♡ 10 3
      ◇ J 8 7 6 5 4  W      E      ◇ A K Q 10 3
      ♣ A K 3           S          ♣ 2
                    ♠ A 8 6 4
                    ♡ K Q J 7
                    ◇ —
                    ♣ Q 9 8 6 4
```

We played this deal against Meckstroth-Rodwell on VuGraph, and there was a lot of drama for the audience before it was over. David opened the South hand 1♡ in third seat, and Jeff overcalled 2◇. I raised to 2♡ (three might have worked better, but we often have a four-card suit in third seat, so that would be a bit much). Eric now risked a nonforcing 2♠! He figured there'd be more bidding, and he wanted to start exploring. However, David passed and Jeff went into a long huddle. The VuGraph audience thought that 2♠ would be the final contract, but Jeff eventually chose to bid 2NT, and several cuebids later they were scoring up 920 in 6◇. Oh, well. Fortunately, it only cost us 2 IMPs, since six of the eight pairs reached 6◇, which I think is a pretty good job.

Only one player, Anton Maas, opened the East hand. He bid 2♠ to show spades and a minor, and when Kirchoff found out the minor was diamonds he keycarded into the slam. Most pairs who reached the slam did so when South opened, West overcalled in diamonds and East splintered in clubs, or cuebid. Stopping in game costs you 9 IMPs.

Dealer South, Both Vul.
E–W Datum +890

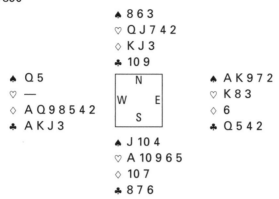

♠ 8 6 3
♡ Q J 7 4 2
◇ K J 3
♣ 10 9

♠ Q 5
♡ —
◇ A Q 9 8 5 4 2
♣ A K J 3

♠ A K 9 7 2
♡ K 8 3
◇ 6
♣ Q 5 4 2

♠ J 10 4
♡ A 10 9 6 5
◇ 10 7
♣ 8 7 6

The best spot is 7♣, which will make against normal breaks in the minors. With bad breaks you might go down in six! In any event, I think that the four pairs who reached 6♣ deserved their 11-IMP gain. Nobody reached 7♣ (win 15 if you did!), and if you try to picture an auction to get there legitimately, you'll see how difficult it is. The first problem is, what should West rebid after 1◇–1♠? Let's see how the eight expert pairs handled this one. Six Wests opened 1◇ and they all heard that 1♠ response. Kirchoff, Vriend and Kaplan both chose to rebid 3◇, which elicited 3NT from partner. At this point Vriend passed and scored 660 after a heart lead, for a 6-IMP loss. Kirchoff and Kaplan continued with 4♣. Wolff raised this to only 5♣ and played there, plus 640 (also losing 6 IMPs). Maas cuebid 4♡ over 4♣ and eventually got to 6♣ to earn the 11-IMP swing.

Koch and Helness both chose to rebid 2♣ after 1◇–1♠. It's a bit of an under-bid, but it gets clubs into the picture and leaves lots of room. Their partners bid 2♡, fourth suit, and both pairs arrived in 6♣ for 1390. Westra chose to jump-shift to 3♣ after 1◇–1♠. His partner raised clubs and later Blackwooded into 6♣. Westra chose not to show his void, or they might have reached seven. At the other two tables West opened artificially and never got to show his clubs. Both pairs ended in 6◇ down one to lose 14 IMPs.

DEAL 13

Dealer South, Neither Vul.
E–W Datum +1200

South opens 3♡.

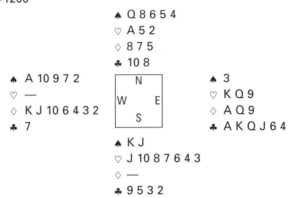

```
                  ♠ Q 8 6 5 4
                  ♡ A 5 2
                  ◇ 8 7 5
                  ♣ 10 8
  ♠ A 10 9 7 2         N          ♠ 3
  ♡ —                             ♡ K Q 9
  ◇ K J 10 6 4 3 2  W   E         ◇ A Q 9
  ♣ 7                  S          ♣ A K Q J 6 4
                  ♠ K J
                  ♡ J 10 8 7 6 4 3
                  ◇ —
                  ♣ 9 5 3 2
```

As you can see from the datum, a fair number of pairs were able to reach the grand slam on this wild deal.

Let's start by looking at the six tables where South opened with 3♡. Branco, Zia, Levy and Meckstroth all chose to overcall 4◇ with the West hand. Chagas and Rodwell both Blackwooded into 7◇ when their partners showed two key-cards and a void. Mouiel and Rosenberg cuebid 4♡ and then had a series of cue-bids to get to 7◇ and 6NT respectively. Ilan Herbst chose to overcall 3♠, which elicited 6♣ from partner to end the auction. Paul Chemla overcalled with 4♡ to show spades and a minor. Perron bid 4NT to ask for the minor, and then over 5◇ he bid 6♣ which sounds like a grand–slam try. However, Chemla, who had already stretched with his 4♡ bid, decided to bid only 6◇ for 940 and a 6-IMP loss.

At the seventh table South opened 2◇, Multi. Manoppo overcalled 2♠, and after North's 3♡ Lasut bid 4♣. Manoppo jumped to 6◇ and Lasut raised to seven, plus 1440. At table eight, the Norwegians passed the South hand (very surprising to me), but they ended up with a huge gain when the Poles had a misunderstanding and played in 4NT (intended as Blackwood) for plus 490, and a 12-IMP loss.

Dealer North, Both Vul.

E–W Datum +2210

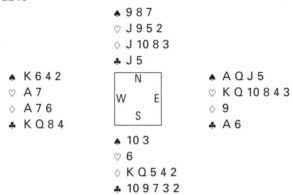

```
                        ♠ 9 8 7
                        ♡ J 9 5 2
                        ◇ J 10 8 3
                        ♣ J 5
        ♠ K 6 4 2          ┌─────────┐      ♠ A Q J 5
        ♡ A 7              │    N    │      ♡ K Q 10 8 4 3
        ◇ A 7 6            │ W     E │      ◇ 9
        ♣ K Q 8 4          │    S    │      ♣ A 6
                           └─────────┘
                        ♠ 10 3
                        ♡ 6
                        ◇ K Q 5 4 2
                        ♣ 10 9 7 3 2
```

O.K. You see the datum. So all eight expert pairs bid and made seven spades. Well done. But wait, not so fast.

Rosenberg, Ofir Herbst, Helgemo and Robson all started with 1♡ and heard partner respond 1♠. In effect, they all splintered and their partners drove to the spade grand. The other four Easts, Kaplan, Meckstroth, Lasut and Berkowitz, all opened with a strong club. Lasut–Manoppo followed with six rounds of natural bidding while Berkowitz and I had six rounds of artificial bidding, both ending in 7♠. Meckstroth–Rodwell also went the artificial route, but ended in 7♡. I suppose they weren't able to determine the major-suit-jack situation. If they had the ♡J, instead of the ♠J, they'd be in a good spot. Anyway, Meckstroth received a diamond lead and played the ♡K and the ♡A, getting the bad news. He was now in dummy to ruff a diamond. Ace and a club to the king let him ruff another diamond. He now needed North to follow to three rounds of spades. His luck was in. He cashed three spades and led dummy's ♣Q. North had to pitch, and Jeff threw his last spade. The lead was in dummy at Trick 12 for the trump coup, plus an exciting 2210.

At the eighth table, Kaplan–Wolff, a first-time pairing, seem to have had some sort of five-level mix-up, ending in 5♠, plus 710. Since the low score got thrown out, the datum was still 2210, but this swung 17 IMPs to Chemla–Perron, and cost Edgar and Bobby the same 17.

DEAL 15

Dealer North, Neither Vul.
E–W Datum +680

North opens 2♡.

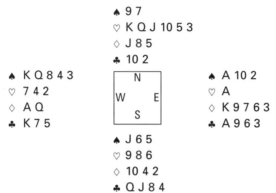

Maybe that North hand would elicit the same 2♡ opening from all eight tables. No chance. Actually seven of the eight Norths opened either 2♡ or Multi 2◊. The other North, Rosenberg, opened 3♡. At that table, Chagas doubled and Branco cuebid 4♡. Chagas bid 4NT (pick-a-minor) and Branco bid 5♠, but Chagas passed, plus 510.

At the seven tables where there was a 2♡ opening or a Multi 2◊, there were seven different auctions! Bridge is an unpredictable game, and I can't see how computers can ever be taught to play it well. How can you program a computer to bid the East-West hands when seven of the world's best pairs all have different inclinations? Two Easts, Kaplan and Rodwell, chose to pass Multi 2◊. South bid 2♡, and Wolff and Meckstroth overcalled 2♠. Kaplan jumped to 6♠, plus 1010, still an 8-IMP gain, whereas Rodwell splintered to 4♡ and then passed 4♠, scoring plus 510 for a 5-IMP loss.

Mouiel and Forrester doubled 2◊ and never got close to slam. At the other three tables, Ofir Herbst, Dennis Koch and Enri Leufkens doubled the 2♡ opening bid. Ilan Herbst responded with a 3♡ cuebid and then jumped to 5♠ after his brother's 4♡. Ofir cuebid 6♡ and Ilan jumped to 7♠, plus 1510 and 13 IMPs for them (minus 13 for Chemla-Perron). Jens Auken had to contend with a 3♡ raise from South, so he jumped directly to 5♠. Koch didn't cuebid 6♡, but simply raised to 6♠. Berry Westra cuebid 3♡, but bid only 4♠ at his next turn, and played there.

Dealer East, E–W Vul.
E–W Datum –220

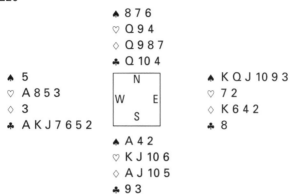

```
                    ♠ 8 7 6
                    ♡ Q 9 4
                    ◇ Q 9 8 7
                    ♣ Q 10 4
   ♠ 5                               ♠ K Q J 10 9 3
   ♡ A 8 5 3          N              ♡ 7 2
   ◇ 3            W       E          ◇ K 6 4 2
   ♣ A K J 7 6 5 2      S            ♣ 8
                    ♠ A 4 2
                    ♡ K J 10 6
                    ◇ A J 10 5
                    ♣ 9 3
```

For the first time in this book the datum is negative, and the winning action was to stop real low. Lasut-Manoppo were the only East-West pair to go plus. Manoppo showed a weak-two in spades (via a Multi 2◇) and Michel Perron doubled. North, Chemla took out to 3◇, passed around to West, Lasut, who doubled! (It appears to me that Lasut's double must have been takeout, but I forgot to ask him in the Hague and I don't know the area code to Manila.) Three diamonds doubled was defeated three tricks, 500 to East-West and 12 IMPs.

Jeff Meckstroth opened with a three-level preempt and played in 3♠ down one to gain 3 IMPs. The 6-1 spade fit plays better than the 7-1 in clubs. The Poles played in spades after East opened on the two-level and then corrected back to 3♠ when West showed clubs. The only other E-W pair to play in spades was Levy-Mouiel, but they were in 4♠ down 200 (win 1). Berkowitz and I, Arnolds-Vriend, Forrester-Robson and Westra-Leufkens played in 3♣, 4♣, 5♣, and 5♣ respectively — down 200, 300, 400 and 400 (win 1, lose 3, and lose 5). Yuk!

DEAL 17

Dealer East, Neither Vul.
E–W Datum +450

*South overcalls hearts
and North raises.*

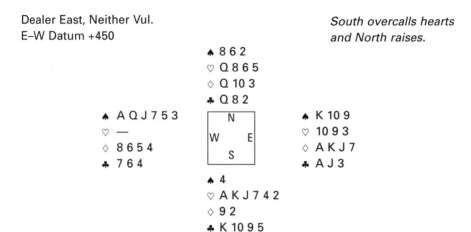

```
                    ♠ 8 6 2
                    ♡ Q 8 6 5
                    ◇ Q 10 3
                    ♣ Q 8 2
  ♠ A Q J 7 5 3      ┌─────────┐      ♠ K 10 9
  ♡ —                │    N    │      ♡ 10 9 3
  ◇ 8 6 5 4          │ W     E │      ◇ A K J 7
  ♣ 7 6 4            │    S    │      ♣ A J 3
                     └─────────┘
                    ♠ 4
                    ♡ A K J 7 4 2
                    ◇ 9 2
                    ♣ K 10 9 5
```

If you and your partner found your way to 6◇, congratulations and 10 IMPs! None of our featured pairs even sniffed at the diamond slam. Six diamonds is excellent without a club lead, just needing diamonds to be 3-2. After a club lead, it needs 3-2 diamonds with the queen onside. For once we have a relatively flat board, all eight pairs bidding and making four spades with an overtrick. However, there were — to no one's surprise by now — eight different auctions!

The various Easts started with either a strong club, a strong notrump or a natural diamond. West showed his spades and on two occasions got pushed to the five-level. Chagas–Branco were the only ones to get past 4♠ on their own. West cuebid 4♡ after East jump-raised 1♠ to three. This caused East to cuebid 5♣, but they subsided in 5♠ and actually needed the fortuitous diamond layout to make this contract.

Dealer North, Both Vul.
E–W Datum +70

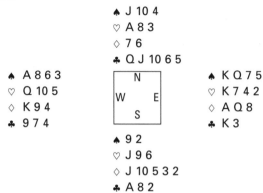

```
                    ♠ J 10 4
                    ♡ A 8 3
                    ◇ 7 6
                    ♣ Q J 10 6 5
  ♠ A 8 6 3        ┌─────────┐      ♠ K Q 7 5
  ♡ Q 10 5         │    N    │      ♡ K 7 4 2
  ◇ K 9 4       W  │         │  E   ◇ A Q 8
  ♣ 9 7 4          │    S    │      ♣ K 3
                   └─────────┘
                    ♠ 9 2
                    ♡ J 9 6
                    ◇ J 10 5 3 2
                    ♣ A 8 2
```

This looks like an easy 620 for E-W in 4♠. There are only two club losers and one heart loser. The problem is that 1NT-3NT is a very likely auction, and it occurred at five tables. All five declarers were down 200 when they got a diamond lead, played on hearts and then lost five club tricks along with 7 IMPs. At the sixth table, where East opened 1NT, the West player, Anton Maas, chose to bid Stayman. This resulted in an 11-IMP swing when 4♠ was reached.

This deal is similar to Hand 6 from this same event. In both cases it was right to play in four-of-a-major, but I'm not convinced that this proves anything. Berkowitz and I and Meckstroth-Rodwell were East-West at the other two tables, and this caused Lasut-Manoppo and Forrester-Robson to lose 12 unlucky IMPs. Unlucky because each time, after East's big club opening, West showed a balanced hand and East bid Stayman, of course. This led to 4♠ and plus 620. Perhaps this is just another example of the random luck involved even in duplicate bridge.

DEAL 19

Dealer South, N–S Vul.
E–W Datum +250

North overcalls in hearts.

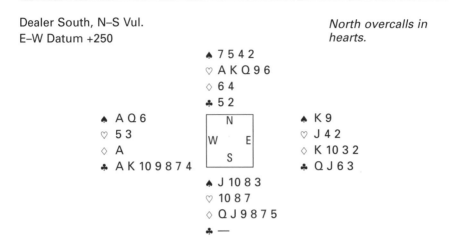

```
                  ♠ 7 5 4 2
                  ♡ A K Q 9 6
                  ◇ 6 4
                  ♣ 5 2
    ♠ A Q 6          N        ♠ K 9
    ♡ 5 3                     ♡ J 4 2
    ◇ A         W      E      ◇ K 10 3 2
    ♣ A K 10 9 8 7 4   S      ♣ Q J 6 3
                  ♠ J 10 8 3
                  ♡ 10 8 7
                  ◇ Q J 9 8 7 5
                  ♣ —
```

Only five of the eight pairs found the correct contract of 5♣ (win 4). As usual, there were five different routes! Ilan Herbst, Carla Arnolds, Gabriel Chagas, Eric Kirchoff and Jeff Meckstroth all opened the West hand 1♣, the last being Precision. North overcalled 1♡, and from then on there was a lot of divergence.

Two Easts doubled (showing both minors), one raised to 2♣ and two others cuebid 2♡. Some got further interference from North-South, others were left alone. Some had two rounds of bidding, others three, others four, but 5♣ was always reached.

Again I ask, "How will computers ever be programmed to play this game?" Berkowitz and I and Levy-Mouiel reached 3NT, but North-South were not amused. They simply cashed their five heart tricks for down one (lose 7). At the eighth table, Geir Helgemo opened the West hand 2♣, strong and artificial, and his partner didn't let him out below 6♣, which was down one on a heart lead (lose 7).

Dealer West, Both Vul.
E–W Datum +660

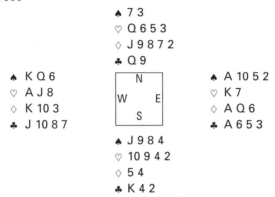

♠ 7 3
♡ Q 6 5 3
◇ J 9 8 7 2
♣ Q 9

♠ K Q 6
♡ A J 8
◇ K 10 3
♣ J 10 8 7

♠ A 10 5 2
♡ K 7
◇ A Q 6
♣ A 6 5 3

♠ J 9 8 4
♡ 10 9 4 2
◇ 5 4
♣ K 4 2

We close this chapter with a bidding and suit-combination problem. How do you play J-10-8-7 opposite A-6-5-3 for one loser? The combination is not listed in the *Official Encyclopedia of Bridge,* and it's hard to come up with a conclusive answer, because a lot depends on what the defense does. Witness the following.

Helgemo–Helness bid 1NT-2♣, 2◇-3♣, 3NT-6NT and received a spade lead from North, Berry Westra. Helgemo won in hand and led the ♣J, covered by the queen and ace. Now he played a low club back to finesse against the nine, but this lost. Because he was in notrump, he'd only have had eleven tricks even with a successful club guess.

If you and your partner reached 6NT, I'll let you pick up the clubs, but you'll still have to score it as minus 100 and a 13-IMP loss. Arnolds-Vriend, Chagas-Branco and Levy-Mouiel also reached slam, but they got to 6♣, which had a much better chance. They all started 1♣-1♠, 1NT and then East invited slam and West, with a maximum, accepted. Levy and Vriend won the heart lead in hand and advanced the ♣J. North played the nine, so the jack lost to the king. Later the club finesse was repeated for a score of 1370. Perhaps North didn't cover because he thought declarer had K-J-10-8 and was intending to go up with the ace and finesse on the way back. I think the Norths will know better next time. Branco did even better by leading the ♣10. This makes it harder for North to cover, but Henry Lasut was right there with the queen. Branco won the ace and led back to his eight, the percentage play, for down one. Two out of three Norths fell from grace, so I'll assume that if you got to 6♣, you'd make it. Assign yourself 1370 and take a 12-IMP gain, but don't gloat about it. The Herbst brothers, Berkowitz and I, Kirchoff-Maas and Meckwell all sniffed at slam but stopped in three or four notrump for a push.

Summary

Well, there you have it. Twenty deals at eight tables and it seems like 160 totally different results! There's always something new and different waiting when the 52 cards are dealt. Maybe the day will come when the world's best players can easily bid to the right contract on all twenty of these deals, but probably not in our lifetime.

Final standings

Zia–Rosenberg	(USA)	+854
Auken–Koch	(Denmark)	+835
Lasut–Manoppo	(Indonesia)	+829
Meckstroth–Rodwell	(USA)	+823
Chagas–Branco	(Brazil)	+822
Levy–Mouiel	(France)	+819
Leufkens–Westra	(Netherlands)	+804
Helgemo–Helness	(Norway)	+767

Rating guide

- **Minus 20 IMPs or more** — You must have bid this set like David and I did.
- **0 to -20 IMPs** — Not bad; after all, you were bidding against datums achieved by sixteen of the best pairs in the world.
- **0 to +20 IMPs** — Well done; your bidding results were better than the average of the participants.
- **Plus 20 IMPs or more** — Maybe you should be invited to this event.

Scoring table

East West datums and vulnerabilities

1. +1110	V		**2.** +670	V
3. +750	NV		**4.** +1110	V
5. +560	NV		**6.** +500	V
7. +360	V		**8.** +100	NV
9. +1120	V		**10.** +1460	V
11. +840	NV		**12.** +890	V
13. +1200	NV		**14.** +2210	V
15. +680	NV		**16.** -220	V
17. +450	NV		**18.** +70	V
19. +250	NV		**20.** +660	V

CAP VOLMAC
1996

The January, 1996 Cap Volmac World Top Tournament was held as usual in The Hague. The victors in a field of 16 pairs were repeat winners, Geir Helgemo and Tor Helness of Norway.

Have you bid the hands on pages 160 and 168 with your favorite partner? Here, from my point of view, are the results of those 15 deals. First, a brief word about the tournament. Imagine superb playing conditions, royal treatment for the players, super-tough competition, splendid ambiance, enthused spectators — and then double that! It's simply a bridge player's dream. David Berkowitz and I were amongst the highest three or four pairs through the first four (of five) sessions, but we had a bad last round and dropped to seventh place. That's an unfortunate place to finish. You see, the top six win cash prizes and automatically get invited back next year.   C'est la vie.

GEIR HELGEMO

TOR HELNESS

Deal 1

Dealer West, Both Vul.
E-W Datum +1430

South bids diamonds.

♠ K 8 7	N	♠ Q J 10 2
♡ A K Q 9 8 6 4	W E	♡ 5 2
◇ 4	S	◇ A K 9
♣ A J		♣ K 7 6 3

Did you reach the excellent heart or notrump slam? If West opens one heart and East responds one spade, South will overcall two diamonds. What should West rebid then? If he jumps to four hearts, his partner probably should take further action, but it's possible to miss the slam. I strongly prefer a two-club opening for West. He's got about nine tricks in his hand, and how bad a description can it be to start two clubs-two diamonds-two hearts? It's not like you can describe this hand better by starting with one heart. Against us, the Danes, Koch-Auken, started one heart-one spade. David overcalled two diamonds and West jumped to four hearts. After long thought, East eventually went right and Blackwooded into the slam for plus 1430. Seven of the eight pairs reached slam, so the datum was +1430. We didn't lose a single IMP. How's that for field protection? For missing the slam you'd lose 13 IMPs.

Dealer West, N-S Vul.
E-W Datum +520

```
        ♠ 4                         ♠ A 7
        ♡ K 10 7        ┌───────┐   ♡ A Q J
        ◇ 9 8 5 4     W │   N   │ E ◇ A K Q 10 7
        ♣ A K 7 6 3     │   S   │   ♣ 10 4 2
                        └───────┘
```

At one table Eric Rodwell opened the West hand one diamond (Precision), and
his partner, Jeff Meckstroth, was able to find out that Eric had four diamonds, one
spade, the ♣A-K and the ♡K. All Eric needed was the ♣Q or 1-4-4-4 shape to
make seven diamonds virtually laydown. So Jeff drove the hand to seven, but was
down one when there was no club miracle (lose 10 IMPs). Actually the clubs
were 5-0, so if you reached the small slam from the East side, they could double
for a club lead and beat you. However, if you reached six diamonds from either
side, take credit for plus 920 (win 9 IMPs). You wouldn't necessarily get doubled
if you reached six diamonds from the East side. I speak from experience. I
opened the East hand two notrump and David bid three spades to show the
minors. I bid four diamonds, and we made several tries for a grand slam before
settling in six. Those grand-slam tries deterred North from making a lead-direct-
ing double of our small slam. Several other pairs reached seven, and one pair
played in three notrump (lose 2 IMPs), so the datum was only +520. If you
reached a club contract, you take only ten tricks for a significant loss.

Deal 3

Dealer East, Both Vul.
E-W Datum +930

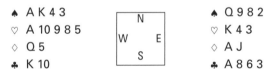

♠ A 9 8 4 2	♠ K Q 6 3
♡ J 5	♡ A K 6
◇ A 2	◇ K 10 6 5
♣ J 8 6 4	♣ K Q

This is an excellent six spades, which will succeed unless trumps are 4-0 or clubs 6-1. That's close to 90%. Only three of the eight tables bid the slam, so the datum was only 930. Most Easts opened two notrump and West didn't even try for slam. I opened with a Precision club (our two-notrump range is 21-22 and I upgraded that beautiful 20 on Deal 2, but not this ugly 20). David responded one spade, showing five or more spades, eight or more points. I bid one notrump, waiting, and he bid two clubs, showing four or more clubs. Just what I needed to hear. Eventually David showed a diamond control and I Blackwooded into the slam, knowing it was almost laydown.

We were surprised to gain 11 IMPs in a field of this caliber. If you got only to 4♠, score yourself minus 6 IMPs.

Deal 4

Dealer West, N-S Vul.
E-W Datum +730

♠ A K 4 3	♠ Q 9 8 2
♡ A 10 9 8 5	♡ K 4 3
◇ Q 5	◇ A J
♣ K 10	♣ A 8 6 3

Six spades by East is quite good, because it requires little more than 3-2 spades. Indeed, spades were 3-2, and hearts were also 3-2, so take plus 980 and 6 IMPs if you reached the slam. Yes, take it even if you got there from the wrong side. The diamond finesse was wrong, and a diamond lead would beat six spades by West, but unless your auction begged for it, there is nothing about the North hand that makes a diamond lead obvious. Six hearts, however, loses a heart and a diamond and 13 IMPs.

We started with a big club and notrump response (9-14 balanced) and settled in four spades to lose 6 IMPs. Natural auctions should start one heart-one spade-three spades, after which East would tend to drive to slam after discovering all the keycards. Do you think he might drive to seven? Switch West's red queen into hearts and the grand slam would be a reasonably good contract.

Dealer North, Both Vul.
E-W Datum +670

South bids spades,
North raises to 3♠ and
South bids 4♠.

♠ J 10	**N**	♠ A 7
♡ 6 3	**W E**	♡ A Q J 7 5
◇ K J 10 7 6 4 3 2	**S**	◇ A 5
♣ 2		♣ A 8 6 3

The heart finesse was wrong (singleton king in fact!), so if you reached six diamonds, assume down one on a spade lead (lose 13 IMPs). Hearts were 5-1, so you should take minus 200 if you reached four hearts (also lose 13). Five diamonds scores 600 (lose 2), and doubling four spades scores 800 and wins 4 IMPs (four aces, two club ruffs).

I opened the East hand a Precision club, and David doubled South's one-spade overcall (showing 5-8 points). I rebid four hearts over North's jump-raise to three spades, and we might have played there. The overcaller, however, was 5-1-2-5 and chose to continue on to four spades. David didn't know if we could make eleven tricks in diamonds, so he chose to defend and we scored our 800. (It was quite surprising to me when he ruffed the second round of clubs!)

Dealer South, Both Vul.
E-W Datum +1130

♠ A 6	**N**	♠ Q 9 8 5
♡ J 8 5 3	**W E**	♡ A K
◇ A K Q 10 8 6	**S**	◇ 7 5 4 3
♣ 8		♣ A 3 2

Six of the eight pairs reached the laydown diamond slam. Most auctions started one diamond-one spade and now West's rebid depended on his opening-bid style. The sound opening bidders rebid only two diamonds, while the light opening bidders had significant extras and could reverse to two hearts or jump to three diamonds.

Against us, the top French pair Levy-Mouel started one diamond-one spade-two diamonds and missed the slam, giving us a juicy 11 IMPs. This form of scoring often metes out undeserved chunks of IMPs (positive or negative!) if you're in the right/wrong place at the right/wrong time. If you bid six diamonds, score up a well-deserved 6 IMPs.

Deal 7

Dealer West, E-W Vul.
E-W Datum +580

*South bids 2♡ and
North 4♡.*

♠ J 5 4
♡ 8 6 3 2
◇ A 3
♣ K Q J 3

♠ K Q 8 3
♡ —
◇ K Q 10 9 8
♣ A 10 7 2

After East opens one diamond and South bids two hearts, West must make a decision. Passing with 11 points is unpalatable, as is making a negative double with only three spades. Maybe three clubs (West is a passed hand), lying only about the club length, is the least of evils.

Against us, Canada's George Mittelman chose to double and, after David's four hearts, Fred Gitelman bid four spades, of course. George wasn't happy, but he eventually passed and was minus 200 when spades were 4-2. (Double dummy four spades might make, but you'll have to live with –200 and a loss of 13 IMPs if you reached it.)

Meckwell reached six spades and went down 400 (lose 14 IMPs). The Danish West passed over two hearts and then jumped to six clubs after his partner doubled the heart raise. This resulted in +1370 for a huge gain on the field (win 13 big ones when many pairs were losing double-figure swings).

Deal 8

Dealer South, Both Vul.
E-W Datum +20

South opens 1◊.

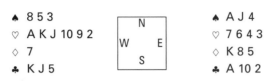

♠ 8 5 3		♠ A J 4
♡ A K J 10 9 2	N W E S	♡ 7 6 4 3
◊ 7		◊ K 8 5
♣ K J 5		♣ A 10 2

Did you reach three notrump by East? Well bid, but sorry, minus 3 IMPs. Hearts were 3-0 offside, and the ◊A was wrong, so no game makes. It was surprising when two North-South pairs had a major defensive accident and allowed four hearts to make. Those two 620s averaged with a bunch of minus 100s and 200s actually gave East-West an average of +20. If you reached four hearts, assume down one (I'll let you guess the club correctly, but that should get you to only nine tricks and a loss of 3 IMPs also). Against us, George Mittelman overcalled one heart as West, and Fred Gitelman cuebid two diamonds. George rebid three hearts to show extras (he might have bid three clubs to show his values) and Fred tried three notrump, ending the auction. I led a diamond from the ◊AQJ98 and Fred was about to claim ten tricks when I showed out on the first heart. Not very fair. He conceded a heart and four diamonds for down one and an unlucky loss of 3 IMPs.

Deal 9

Dealer South, Neither Vul.
E-W Datum +920

South passes and then bids spades. North raises to 4♠.

♠ 7		♠ 8 5 4
♡ A J 10 9	N W E S	♡ K Q
◊ K 9 6 3 2		◊ A Q J 8 7
♣ K 9 8		♣ A 5 3

Seven out of the eight pairs reached six diamonds, so the best you can do on this deal is break even against the datum of +920. We started one diamond-two diamonds, inverted. If anything, the interference helped us, because East's three small spades fit well opposite West's presumed shortness. Without inverted minors, East would have to make up a response, perhaps two clubs. Alternatively, he might bid three clubs, which some partnerships use as an artificial forcing diamond raise. In either case, reaching slam would simply be a matter of diagnosing West's spade shortness.

If you accidentally doubled four spades, take +100 and lose 13 IMPs (South was 5-1-1-6). Bidding only five diamonds loses you 11 IMPs.

Deal 10

Dealer West, Neither Vul.
E-W Datum +440

♠ J 4 2   ♠ Q 6
♡ —   ♡ A 9
◇ A K Q 9 8 6 4   ◇ 7 5
♣ Q J 5   ♣ A K 10 9 8 4 3

Don't let the datum fool you. Against us Henky Lasut opened the West hand three notrump, gambling, and Eddie Manoppo jumped to five diamonds and scored 440 on a heart lead. However, this board was not 'flat' at 440. Koch-Auken were +1440 in seven clubs on a heart lead. There were also two 940s, and some –50s and –300s East-West.

If you reached a slam, assume a spade lead and lose 10 IMPs. You don't think that's fair? Well, I'll offer you a deal. Since the ♠A is to the left of the opening bidder, I'll assume he'd lead it against a slam, but if you are lucky enough to reach slam from the East side, South would probably lead a heart from the ♡K-Q-J, so take your ill-deserved +940 (win 11 IMPs) or +1440 (win 14 IMPs).

Deal 11

Dealer West, N-S Vul.
E-W Datum +470

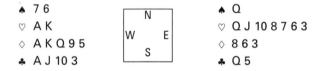

♠ 7 6   ♠ Q
♡ A K   ♡ Q J 10 8 7 6 3
◇ A K Q 9 5   ◇ 8 6 3
♣ A J 10 3   ♣ Q 5

The club finesse was on and everything split well, so six hearts from either side would produce +980 and win you 11 IMPs. We started with a big club and received a little interference (they wouldn't come in over anything other than a big club). In any event, we never got close to this slam, but were relieved to get a 'push' when no one in the field reached the six-level and the datum was only +470.

If West opens two notrump, I don't think East is necessarily worth anything more than a sign-off at a heart game. Perhaps West should upgrade his hand and open two clubs intending to rebid two notrump. Now East might make a noise, and if he can transfer to hearts and show spade shortness, that is just what West would need to hear.

Deal 12

Dealer East, N-S Vul.
E-W Datum +980

```
♠ 7 6                    ♠ A K 2
♡ K 10 9 5 3             ♡ Q J 8
◇ A 10 9 8 6 4           ◇ K 2
♣ —                      ♣ A 9 6 4 3
```

On the previous deal it surprised me that no one reached slam. On this deal I was just as surprised that all but one pair were in six hearts. Both red suits split 3-2 so there was nothing to the play. If East opens one notrump, will West really be thinking of slam? No, but if he shows both red suits, East will have the best-looking strong notrump in the history of bridge and might just ask for keycards and drive to the heart slam.

We again started with a big club, and West revealed a game force with both red suits. It was now trivial for East to Blackwood into the slam, but alas, it was for no gain on the deal. Stopping in game costs 11 IMPs.

Deal 13

Dealer West, Both Vul.
E-W Datum –170

```
♠ 9 8 3                  ♠ A K 10
♡ 3                      ♡ A 9 5
◇ 5 3 2                  ◇ A K 9 8 4
♣ A Q 10 9 7 3           ♣ J 5
```

This is a real toughie! The best IMP contract is five clubs. Six clubs isn't bad, but it would fail because the club finesse was wrong (lose 7 IMPs). Three notrump also fails, in fact, by two tricks, after the obvious heart lead, and costs you 9 IMPs. Score +600 and win 13 IMPs if you somehow got to five clubs, but we presume most pairs bid 2NT–3NT (as our opponents did) or 1◇–1NT, 2NT. Of course, you'd survive in three notrump if the clubs came in, but that's only about a 50% chance. Any North at this level of competition will hold up the ♣K if it's offside, even if it's doubleton!

Deal 14

Dealer North, Both Vul.
E-W Datum +1390

<pre>
        ♠ K 10 7 6   ┌─────┐   ♠ A 5
        ♡ A 9 2   │ N │   ♡ K J
        ◇ A K 10 9 2   W │   │ E   ◇ Q J 7 5
        ♣ 4   │ S │   ♣ A J 10 8 3
                           └─────┘
</pre>

Again, no one in the field reached the top spot, this time seven diamonds (win 13 IMPs if you did). One East-West pair reached three notrump (lose 13 IMPs as you deserve), and the other seven (of which we were one) reached only six diamonds for zero swing. I chose one notrump with the East hand, and David showed a game force with diamonds. I found out we had all the keycards, but no ♣K, so I settled for the small slam. Seven is pretty easy to play. Win the (say) trump lead with the ace, cash the five side-suit winners, ruff a heart low, ruff a club low, and then claim on a high cross-ruff. This loses only to 6-1 clubs or 6-2 hearts the wrong way. Can you do better?

Deal 15

Dealer North, Neither Vul.
E-W Datum +610

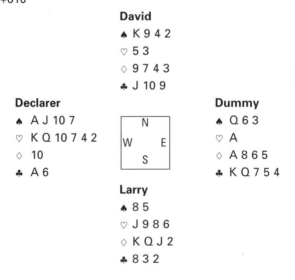

<pre>
                        David
                        ♠ K 9 4 2
                        ♡ 5 3
                        ◇ 9 7 4 3
                        ♣ J 10 9

        Declarer   Dummy
        ♠ A J 10 7   ┌─────┐   ♠ Q 6 3
        ♡ K Q 10 7 4 2 │ N │   ♡ A
        ◇ 10   W │   │ E   ◇ A 8 6 5
        ♣ A 6   │ S │   ♣ K Q 7 5 4
                        └─────┘
                        Larry
                        ♠ 8 5
                        ♡ J 9 8 6
                        ◇ K Q J 2
                        ♣ 8 3 2
</pre>

This was from the last match and left a particularly sour taste in our mouths. We were in fifth place playing against the third-place Dutch pair, Muller-DeBoer. East chose to open one notrump and West showed 4-6 in the majors with slam interest. East jumped to six spades, and David had to choose an opening lead. Naturally, he led a club.

A diamond lead would have sealed declarer's fate. David could win his ♠K and shorten declarer with another diamond play. This would lead to down several tricks. Their auction started one notrump-two clubs-two diamonds, so I could have doubled two diamonds for a diamond lead, but I don't like scores such as minus 960 (two diamonds redoubled making four). Unfortunately, we tend to lead from J-10-9 as opposed to 9-7-4-3, so declarer won David's club lead with the ace, crossed to the ♡A and played the ♠Q. David ducked this and won the next spade finesse to belatedly play a diamond. Declarer won, drew trumps, tried the hearts and then fell back on the clubs, taking three spades, three hearts, one diamond and five clubs for plus 980 and 9 IMPs. If David ducked the second spade as well, declarer would probably smell a rat — just look at the ♠8, which gives away the show (South would cover with the ♠K-9-8-x). Even if declarer did want to try another spade finesse, he'd be okay if he crossed in clubs, not diamonds, to take it. When South shows out, he could win the ♠A, cash the high hearts throwing dummy's diamond losers, and give North his trump trick.

This loss of 9 IMPs on the last board dropped us from 5th place to 7th. We could have been saved by one of our American buddies who reached seven clubs against the 7th-place pair. He got a trump lead and had to assume trumps were 3-3 if he were to have any chance. This gives him one spade, three hearts, one diamond, five clubs, and a diamond ruff in the short club hand for 11 sure tricks. He had to decide on either a spade finesse or 4-2 hearts for his extra tricks. Because my hand had overcalled one diamond, declarer opted for the spade finesse, instead of the more likely 4-2 hearts. Down one instead of making seven affected the datum score and six of the seven top overall places.

Anyone for six hearts? That's a good contract, and if you reached it you fully deserve your +980 and 9 IMPs. Six notrump gets you –100 (lose 12), and for six spades take 980 from the West side only, otherwise –100.

Summary

Final standings

Helgemo-Helness	(Norway)	+131
Lasut-Manoppo	(Indonesia)	+112
Muller-DeBoer	(Netherlands)	+98
Zia-Rosenberg	(USA)	+61
Buratti-Lanzarotti	(Italy)	+26
Leufkens-Westra	(Netherlands)	+22
Berkowitz-Cohen	(USA)	+16
Chemla-Cronier	(France)	0

Rating guide

- **Minus 20 IMPs or more** — Need to work on your slam bidding.
- **0 to -20 IMPs — Not bad**. After all, you were bidding against datums achieved by the Top Sixteen.
- **0 to +20 IMPs** — Well done. Your bidding results were better than the participants in The Hague.
- **Plus 20 IMPs or more** — Maybe you should be invited to next year's tournament.

Scoring table

East-West datums and vulnerabilities

1. +1430	V		**2.** +520	NV
3. +930	V		**4.** +730	NV
5. +670	V		**6.** +1130	V
7. +580	V		**8.** +20	V
9. +920	NV		**10.** +440	NV
11. +470	NV		**12.** +980	NV
13. -170	V		**14.** +1390	V
15. +610	NV			

CAP GEMINI
1997

This year's World Top Tournament was as good as ever. The 11th edition, this time sponsored by computer software giant Cap Gemini, was held at the beautiful Hotel Des Indes in the Hague.

Sixteen world-class pairs from twelve different countries (Brazil, Canada, China, France, Holland, Indonesia, Italy, Norway, Pakistan, Poland, Taiwan and the United States) were invited. As usual, try bidding the hands on pages 161 and 169 with your favorite partner (or by yourself) and compare your results to those achieved in the Netherlands.

GABRIEL CHAGAS

MARCELO BRANCO

Deal 1

Dealer West, Both Vul.
N-S Datum +1640

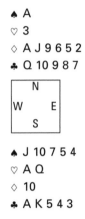

```
            ♠ A
            ♡ 3
            ◇ A J 9 6 5 2
            ♣ Q 10 9 8 7
               ┌─────────┐
               │    N    │
               │ W     E │
               │    S    │
               └─────────┘
            ♠ J 10 7 5 4
            ♡ A Q
            ◇ 10
            ♣ A K 5 4 3
```

On Deal 1 we were in the wrong place at the wrong time. Jeff Meckstroth and
Eric Rodwell bid scientifically and accurately against us to the right spot:

JEFF	ERIC
NORTH	SOUTH
1◇	1♠
2♡[1]	2♠[2]
3♣[3]	4♡[4]
5◇[5]	7♣

    1. Artificial

    2. Asking

    3. 5+-5+ maximum (for a limited opening)

    4. RKCB for clubs

    5. Two keycards + ♣Q

There were no awful breaks, so thirteen tricks were easy. Notice Jeff's decision to treat his hand as a maximum. Bidding and making 7♣ for 2140 was an
11-IMP again against the datum score of 1640. The only other pairs to reach the
grand were Zia–Levin and French world champions Levy–Mari.

    I think that after 1◇–1♠, 2♣, the South hand should already be thinking of
big things. When he finds out about the fifth club, he should know that even
opposite an awful hand, the grand rates to be at worst on a finesse (as long as all
the keycards are present). But pairs from Brazil, Holland, Italy, Poland and Taiwan
surprisingly all stopped in 6♣ and lost 6 IMPs.

Dealer West, Both Vul.
N–S Datum +510

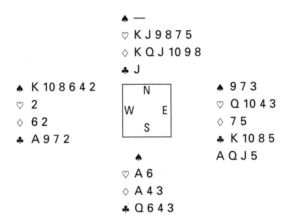

```
                    ♠ —
                    ♡ K J 9 8 7 5
                    ◇ K Q J 10 9 8
                    ♣ J
    ♠ K 10 8 6 4 2        N            ♠ 9 7 3
    ♡ 2             W           E      ♡ Q 10 4 3
    ◇ 6 2                 S            ◇ 7 5
    ♣ A 9 7 2                          ♣ K 10 8 5
                    ♠                  A Q J 5
                    ♡ A 6
                    ◇ A 4 3
                    ♣ Q 6 4 3
```

On Deal 2 it's worth being in 6◇. Without a club lead it is virtually laydown, and after a club lead it needs nothing more than 3-2 hearts. The full deal shows that a club lead would probably defeat the contract. Double-dummy, even after a club lead, the contract can be made by the unlikely line of drawing two rounds of trumps and then leading the ♡J. If East ducks, let it run, and if he covers, cross back to the ♡K and take a ruffing finesse for the 10. This line is a little more attractive if West, the dealer, opens with 2♠. At our table, West passed and we bid as follows:

LARRY	DAVID
NORTH	SOUTH
1♡	1♠
2◇	3♣
3◇	3NT
4♡	pass

Perhaps I should have bid 4◇ at my third or fourth turn. Three pairs stopped in game and five reached slam. One of the slams was 6♡ by Huang-Kuo, down 200. Only two of the four pairs in 6◇ made it, so the datum was plus 510. I think good bidding should be rewarded, and 2 out of 4 is not enough of a sample to convince me that the slam would go down, so if you reached 6◇, take 1370 and score up a gain of 13 IMPs. If you stopped in 4♡, assume 620 (win 3), and for 5◇, assume 620 also and win 3. For 3NT, take 600, but don't be proud of your 3-IMP gain.

Deal 3

Dealer East, E–W Vul.
N–S Datum +370

West bids spades.

♠ A 10 5 2
♡ K 3
◇ Q J 10 7 2
♣ 6 4

♠ J 9 7
♡ A
◇ A K 9 8 6
♣ A 10 8 7

The datum was 370, because most of the field (6 out of 8) stopped safely in 5◇. Only France's Bompis–Szwarc reached the doomed slam (lose 10 IMPs). At the last table, Martens–Szymanowski of Poland collected only 200 against 4♡ doubled and lost 5 IMPs. Assume eleven tricks if you played in diamonds or notrump, and win 6 and 7 IMPs respectively.

Dealer East, E–W Vul.
N–S Datum +830

```
          ♠ A
          ♡ J 10 8 7 2
          ◊ K Q 6
          ♣ A J 5 3
        ┌─────────┐
        │    N    │
        │ W     E │
        │    S    │
        └─────────┘
          ♠ K 10 3
          ♡ A 6
          ◊ A J 10 5 3 2
          ♣ Q 10
```

On the fourth deal, only two pairs missed the excellent diamond slam, so the datum was 830. If you reached 7◊, you're down one (the ♣K was wrong) and you lose 14 IMPs. In 6◊, you can't help but take twelve tricks and gain 11 IMPs; on a heart lead (from doubleton nine) you can set up hearts to pitch your club loser. If you reached 6NT (win 12 IMPs) or 3NT (lose 4 IMPs), you also take twelve tricks. Levy–Mari and Kokish–Gitelman stopped in 3NT.

David and I reached 3◊. Does that seem hard to believe? Notice that I didn't say we stopped in three diamonds. This was our auction:

DAVID	LARRY
South	North
1◊	1♡
1NT	2◊[1]
3◊	?

1. Game–forcing checkback

As I was thinking over 3◊, we all heard a comment from the next table, 'Making six'. The boards are played simultaneously, and it is surprising that this kind of thing doesn't happen more often. Even though the playing area is spacious, there is still a chance of overhearing another table. We called the director, and he ruled that we shouldn't play the board. He awarded us +3 IMPs and our opponents +3 IMPs. Now I know how to win this event. Just tell the director that we've overheard the next table on all 150 deals, and score +450 IMPs to win by a landslide.

Deal 5

Dealer South, N–S Vul.
N–S Datum +140

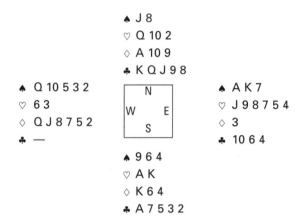

```
                        ♠ J 8
                        ♡ Q 10 2
                        ◊ A 10 9
                        ♣ K Q J 9 8
      ♠ Q 10 5 3 2     ┌─────────┐     ♠ A K 7
      ♡ 6 3            │    N    │     ♡ J 9 8 7 5 4
      ◊ Q J 8 7 5 2    │ W     E │     ◊ 3
      ♣ —              │    S    │     ♣ 10 6 4
                        └─────────┘
                        ♠ 9 6 4
                        ♡ A K
                        ◊ K 6 4
                        ♣ A 7 5 3 2
```

The fifth deal produced a different scenario at all eight tables. First, so you can score yourselves, assume a spade lead. You go plus 600 in 5♣ and win 10 IMPs (well bid!), or, more likely I suspect, minus 100 in 3NT (lose 6 IMPs). In the latter case you'd be in the good company of seven out of eight world–class pairs. I presented this problem with no interference, as was the case at half the tables. It's true that if the opponents bid spades, you'd be more likely to avoid 3NT; that happened when Bompis-Szwarc were the only pair to reach 5♣.

At our table, South opened a Precision diamond. We passed throughout (they bid 1◊-2♣-3♣-3NT), and David judged well to lead a high spade from ace-king third. At some tables South opened 1NT and North raised to 3NT, but all the Wests found the spade lead rather than a diamond. At other tables North played 3NT after West had bid diamonds. In that case it was very difficult for East to lead a spade, but Gabriel Chagas found the spade lead after 1♣-(2◊ over-call)-3NT.

Dealer North, Both Vul.
N–S Datum +270

<pre>
              ♠ A 5 4
              ♡ A Q 5
              ◇ A J 7 2
              ♣ J 10 7
            ┌─────────┐
            │   N   │
            │ W   E │
            │   S   │
            └─────────┘
              ♠ K 10
              ♡ K 9 6 4 2
              ◇ K 6 4 3
              ♣ 6 3
</pre>

The datum here was 270, because half the field reached 4♡ making (win 8 IMPs), and half reached 3NT down one on a club lead when clubs broke 5–3 (lose 9 IMPs). Everyone started with a strong notrump and South transferred to hearts, then offered North a choice. Ideally, South's second bid would be a natural, game-forcing 3◇. This would keep North from considering notrump. However, several Souths bid 3NT at their second turn and North passed.

Facing only a 14–16 notrump, I didn't want to force to game, so I rebid 2NT with the South hand, and David guessed to bid the game in notrump. Notice that if one of my small diamonds had been a small club, he'd have chosen the better contract. Meckstroth and Rodwell produced the best auction, because they had one of their millions of gadgets available. South transferred to hearts and then bid 2♠, artificial. Opener asked and was able to discover that 4♡ was the right contract.

Deal 7

Dealer West, Both Vul.
N–S Datum +210

East bids spades.

♠ 9
♡ A Q J 7 6 5
◊ A 7 6
♣ K Q 8

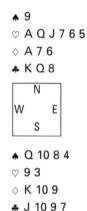

♠ Q 10 8 4
♡ 9 3
◊ K 10 9
♣ J 10 9 7

Deal 7 shows how powerful tens and nines can be. Game, especially 3NT, is excellent after East's spade overcall. In fact, 3NT is unbeatable (the overcaller has the ♠J), and you should also assume you'd make game in hearts, since it would probably make at the table. Against us, the Chinese ladies reached 3NT for a good pickup:

	MING		**WANG**
WEST	NORTH	EAST	SOUTH
pass	1♣[1]	1♠	pass
pass	dbl	pass	2NT
pass	3♡	pass	3NT
all pass			

1. Precision.

The datum was 210, because only two pairs bid and made game. Assume ten tricks in hearts or nine tricks in notrump, and win 9 IMPs in either case. For defending one-spade doubled, assume plus 200 for a push.

Dealer North, Neither Vul.
N–S Datum +830

```
              ♠ K
              ♡ A Q J 8 3
              ◇ A Q 9 3
              ♣ Q 7 4
            ┌─────────┐
            │    N    │
            │ W     E │
            │    S    │
            └─────────┘
              ♠ Q 7 6 3
              ♡ 9
              ◇ K J 6 5 4 2
              ♣ A J
```

Six of eight pairs reached the excellent diamond slam. If you reached it from the normal South seat, it is cold; even a club lead won't bother you. But from the North seat (maybe 1♡-1♠, 2◇), it still makes, because the ♣K is right, so take your 11 IMPs either way. There are nine tricks in notrump on a spade lead (lose 6 IMPs) and twelve tricks in diamonds from either side, so bidding only five diamonds costs you 5 IMPs.

Deal 9

Dealer North, E–W Vul.
N–S Datum +340

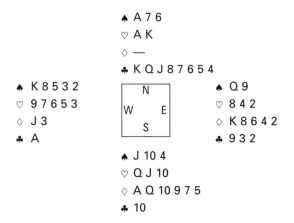

```
                        ♠ A 7 6
                        ♡ A K
                        ◇ —
                        ♣ K Q J 8 7 6 5 4
      ♠ K 8 5 3 2          ┌─────────┐        ♠ Q 9
      ♡ 9 7 6 5 3          │    N    │        ♡ 8 4 2
      ◇ J 3             W  │       E │        ◇ K 8 6 4 2
      ♣ A                  │    S    │        ♣ 9 3 2
                           └─────────┘
                        ♠ J 10 4
                        ♡ Q J 10
                        ◇ A Q 10 9 7 5
                        ♣ 10
```

The ninth deal was a test for both North-South and East-West. First, North-South had to reach 3NT instead of a club game or slam. We bid as follows:

West	**DAVID** NORTH	EAST	**LARRY** SOUTH
	1♣[1]	pass	2◇
pass	3♣	pass	3◇
pass	3♡	pass	3♠[2]
dbl	pass	pass	3NT
all pass			

1. Precision.
2. Stalling.

I suppose we were a bit lucky that five or six clubs has such problems. When 5♣ was reached, it could have been easily defeated by a spade lead. After the ♠Q lead, declarer must eventually suffer a spade ruff. Many Easts, however, led a heart or a club. When West took his ♣A he shifted to a low spade. We can all see that declarer can survive this by rising with the ace, cashing some clubs and high hearts, and then exiting with a spade. In practice, the Norths ducked the spade return to East's queen, and East returned a spade to let the contract make.

Bauke Muller and Wubbo deBoer of the Netherlands were the only pair to find the winning defense. Muller led a trump and deBoer switched to a spade, ducked to the queen. Now East exited safely with another trump, and declarer had to lose a spade at the end for down one. Nicely defended!

If you reached five (or six) clubs, assume eleven tricks, a gift from your author; so win 2 IMPs for game or lose 9 IMPs for bidding the slam. If you reached 3NT, well done, and assume 460 (win 3 IMPs). We were disappointed that the datum was as high as 340; we were hoping for more failed club contracts.

Deal 10

Dealer East, Both Vul.
N–S Datum +620

```
              ♠ 10
              ♡ K 10 7
              ◇ A K 7 3 2
              ♣ K 10 7 6
            ┌──────────┐
            │     N    │
            │ W      E │
            │     S    │
            └──────────┘
              ♠ A K 8 3 2
              ♡ 2
              ◇ J 10 5 4
              ♣ A 5 3
```

If you reached 5◇, you did very well. Even if you lose a diamond trick, you'll make your game; the same can't be said for 3NT on a heart lead. Since you need to know your score, you'll have to decide how to play the diamonds if you reached 3NT or 6◇. In both cases, with no opposition bidding, you get a heart lead and continuation. Well, what now? Maybe you want to go against the odds and finesse in 3NT, because you know that some pairs will be in 6◇ making if diamonds are 2-2?

It turns out that three pairs played 3NT, two played in 5◇, and three played in 6◇. One of the slammers and one of the three notrumpers finessed and went down. The other six declarers successfully played for the drop and the Q-x was doubleton offside. This all averaged out to make the datum 620.

So take zero for bidding 5◇, and be honest about your play in diamonds in alternative contracts. If you played for the drop, take +13 IMPs for the slam and zero for 3NT. If you were a finesser, I'm afraid you lose 12 IMPs in either contract.

Deal 11

Dealer East, Neither Vul.
N–S Datum +460

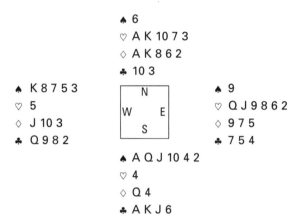

```
                        ♠ 6
                        ♡ A K 10 7 3
                        ◇ A K 8 6 2
                        ♣ 10 3
        ♠ K 8 7 5 3        ┌─────────┐        ♠ 9
        ♡ 5               │    N    │        ♡ Q J 9 8 6 2
        ◇ J 10 3         │ W     E │        ◇ 9 7 5
        ♣ Q 9 8 2        │    S    │        ♣ 7 5 4
                         └─────────┘
                        ♠ A Q J 10 4 2
                        ♡ 4
                        ◇ Q 4
                        ♣ A K J 6
```

On this deal, the only pair to reach the top spot of 6NT were French internationals Bompis–Szwarc, but they kind of backed into it when they were faced with a bizarre Dutch preempt:

	SZWARC		**BOMPIS**
WEST	NORTH	EAST	SOUTH
		2♣[1]	dbl
pass	3♣	pass	3♠
pass	4◇	pass	5♣
pass	5♡	pass	5NT
pass	6♡	pass	6♠
pass	6NT	all pass	

1. Game forcing, or 0–5 any shape.

It's hard to say that they were on firm footing, but the French scored 990 and won 11 IMPs against the 460 datum. Our opponents were a bit unlucky; while the rest of field stopped in 4♠, China's Che Hung Kuo and Patrick Huang reached the excellent spade slam:

HUANG	**KUO**
NORTH	SOUTH
	1♠
2♡	3♣
3◇	3♠
4◇	5♠
6♠	

If spades split, there were twelve top tricks, but the 5-1 break gave us a lucky +50 and an 11-IMP gain. Of course, 6NT is the best spot, because if spades don't behave you have the extra chance of 3-3 diamonds, which was there. So take 450 (zero) or 490 (win 1) if you bid game, and take 990 (11 IMPs) for 6NT (well done!) or -50 for 6♠ (lose 10 — sometimes bridge can be so unfair).

Deal 12

Dealer East, E–W Vul.
N–S Datum +930

```
            ♠ A J 2
            ♡ J 9
            ◊ K 7
            ♣ A K Q J 9 7
```

```
            ♠ K 6
            ♡ K Q
            ◊ A J 9 8 5 4
            ♣ 8 5 3
```

Deal 12 is similar to Deal 11 in that more than one slam is excellent, but some are more excellent than others. As you can see, there are only eleven top tricks in 6NT. You need a spade or diamond finesse or a squeeze for the twelfth. Six diamonds is the worst slam; it needs 3-2 diamonds with the queen onside. The best contract, reached by six of the eight pairs, is 6♣. This gives you tons of extra chances by ruffing a spade or setting up diamonds for twelve tricks.

As the cards lay, you'd succeed in 6NT or 6♣ but fail in 6◊. Poland's Martens–Szymanowski were slightly lucky to win 2 IMPs for 990 (against the 930 datum) for their 6NT, and Brazil's Chagas–Branco were even luckier to win 10 IMPs when Kokish–Gitelman reached only 5◊ against them. We reached 6♣ for no swing. If you bid 6◊, you lose 14 IMPs.

Deal 13

Dealer South, Both Vul.
N–S Datum +910

*West bids hearts and
East jump-raises.*

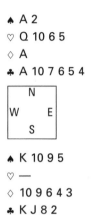

♠ A 2
♥ Q 10 6 5
♦ A
♣ A 10 7 6 5 4

♠ K 10 9 5
♥ —
♦ 10 9 6 4 3
♣ K J 8 2

This deal was poorly managed by the expert field, as only three pairs reached the club slam. We bid the hands as follows:

	DAVID		**LARRY**
WEST	NORTH	EAST	SOUTH
			pass
1♥	2♣	3♥	4♥
dbl	6♣	all pass	

Perhaps David should have passed 4♥ doubled to see if I could redouble to show first-round control. Then we might have reached seven. Seven happens to make because diamonds are 4–3 and the ♣Q is singleton, but six is quite high enough. Here it was worth 10 IMPs.

Many Souths jumped to 5♣ or made a responsive double with my hand over the 3♥ raise. Obviously, I preferred 4♥, and was rewarded with a surprising 10-IMP gain against the 910 datum. Assume thirteen tricks in any club contract (lose 7 IMPs for 5♣, win 15 IMPs for 7♣), nine tricks in notrump (lose 7 IMPs for 3NT), and six tricks on defense if you defended 3♥ doubled (lose 9 IMPs).

Dealer East, E–W Vul.
N–S Datum +620

East deals and opens
1◊ ; West passes.

♠ —
♡ K Q
◊ A K Q 5 2
♣ K Q J 8 6 5

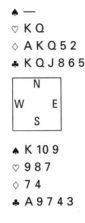

♠ K 10 9
♡ 9 8 7
◊ 7 4
♣ A 9 7 4 3

The North hand looks like a *Bridge World* Master Solvers' Club headache. I was the only player as North to face the auction 1◊-pass-pass, which is the auction I presented to you as the problem. At most tables it went 1◊-pass-1♠ to my hand. Perhaps I should have passed out 1◊; a trump lead would result in our scoring down five, plus 500. But I didn't want to give up on 920, so I elected not to pass. Perhaps I should have doubled, or tried 2♣, but I bid a straightforward 5♣, and now it was up to David. After some thought, he passed and we lost 5 IMPs.

This was another deal where the auction was different at all eight tables. Some Norths overcalled 2♣ after 1◊-pass-1♠ and were surprised to hear a club raise from partner. Over that raise, it's tempting to bid 5♠ (Exclusion Key Card Blackwood) and try for seven, but it turns out that only three of the eight pairs reached even the small slam.

Deal 15

Dealer North, E–W Vul.
N–S Datum +690

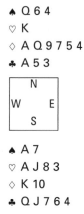

♠ Q 6 4
♡ K
♢ A Q 9 7 5 4
♣ A 5 3

♠ A 7
♡ A J 8 3
♢ K 10
♣ Q J 7 6 4

Only half the field reached the good diamond slam on this deal. Against us on VuGraph the Dutch bid as follows:

WESTRA	LEUFKENS
NORTH	SOUTH
1♢	2♣
3♢	4♢
4♡	4♠
5♣	5♡
6♢	pass

I can't say that I'm thrilled with their auction, especially that 3♢ rebid on ace-queen sixth. Playing 2/1 as game forcing or promising a rebid, the auction is much easier, since North can rebid 2♢. The cards were extremely friendly, and there was no way to beat either 6♣ or 6♢. The only slam that would fail is 6NT by South on a spade lead. So assume twelve tricks in either minor, eleven tricks in notrump by South, and twelve tricks in notrump by North, and score as follows: lose 2 for 5♢ or 5♣; win 6 for 6♣ or 6♢; lose 6 for 3NT by South, and lose 5 for 3NT by North; lose 12 IMPs for 6NT by South, but win 7 for 6NT by North.

Dealer East, N–S Vul.
N–S Datum +440

```
              ♠ 6 5 4 3
              ♡ A 8 3
              ◇ K 9 8 6 4
              ♣ A
            ┌─────────┐
            │    N    │
            │ W     E │
            │    S    │
            └─────────┘
              ♠ 7 2
              ♡ J 7 6
              ◇ A Q
              ♣ K Q J 7 3 2
```

On Deal 16 we lost 8 IMPs due to either poor bidding or poor judgment.
You be the judge:

DAVID	LARRY
NORTH	SOUTH
	2♣[1]
2◇[2]	3♣[3]
pass	

1. 11–15, 6+ clubs.
2. Forcing artificial inquiry.
3. Minimum, no four–card major.

I hated to show a minimum, but since I was second-seat vulnerable (the soundest position), I chose to go the low route. David's final pass was pretty automatic, I think, yet there were nine easy tricks when spades proved to be 4-3. At some tables the auction went 1♣-1♠, 2♣-2NT, 3NT. At the tables where North responded 1◇, the Easts overcalled 1♠ with ♠AKJ10. This kept North-South out of 3NT. Half the field was in 3NT, and half in 3♣. Both contracts made exactly nine tricks.

If you reached 5♣, assume the defense attacks hearts early and you are down two for a loss of 11 IMPs. Getting to 3NT is worth 4 IMPs, while stopping in 3♣ loses you 8.

Deal 17

Dealer North, Neither Vul.
N–S Datum +30

> ♠ A K 9 5
> ♡ 10 9 3
> ◇ A K 5 4
> ♣ K J

> ♠ J 8 7 6 4 2
> ♡ A Q 7 6
> ◇ —
> ♣ Q 8 2

When we played this one, David opened the North hand with a Precision club, and East overcalled a natural diamond. This probably made the heart finesse more of a favorite, in which case we did well to bid 6♠. The slam needs 2–1 spades and the heart finesse. Good news for us, the heart finesse was right. Bad news, the spades were 3–0 (offside — not that you'd guess them even if they were onside, although leading the jack is a good idea anyway), so stopping in game gets you 9 IMPs against the datum of 30. Only two of the eight pairs avoided the slightly–below–average slam. Bidding the slam only costs you a 2–IMP loss.

Dealer South, Neither Vul.
N–S Datum +120

West cuebids to show majors and East bids 2♡.

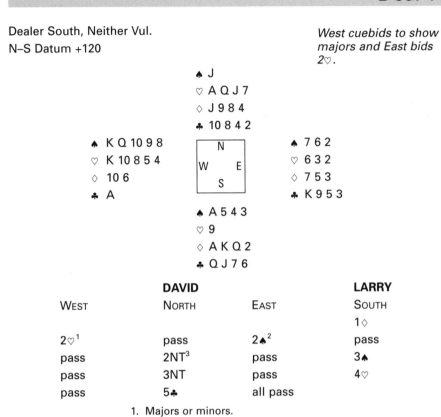

```
                    ♠ J
                    ♡ A Q J 7
                    ◇ J 9 8 4
                    ♣ 10 8 4 2
   ♠ K Q 10 9 8          N          ♠ 7 6 2
   ♡ K 10 8 5 4                      ♡ 6 3 2
   ◇ 10 6          W         E       ◇ 7 5 3
   ♣ A                  S           ♣ K 9 5 3
                    ♠ A 5 4 3
                    ♡ 9
                    ◇ A K Q 2
                    ♣ Q J 7 6
```

	DAVID		**LARRY**
WEST	NORTH	EAST	SOUTH
			1◇
2♡[1]	pass	2♠[2]	pass
pass	2NT[3]	pass	3♠
pass	3NT	pass	4♡
pass	5♣	all pass	

1. Majors or minors.
2. Pass or correct.
3. Takeout.

On Deal 18 we were on the right side of the luck when we were able to take eleven tricks in a somewhat pushy game.

After David's 2NT, I cuebid twice with visions of slam opposite as little as

$$♠ x \quad ♡ x x x \quad ◇ J x x x \quad ♣ A K x x x$$

David won the spade lead and played a club to West's ace. The spade return was ruffed, followed by a diamond to dummy and another spade ruff. Now David played his last club, the ten, and East ducked his king. David crossed in diamonds, drove out the high trump, won the diamond return, drew trumps, and took a heart finesse (actually it showed up) for his eleventh trick.

Assume eleven tricks in five of either minor (5◇ is tricky, but I'm feeling generous) for a gain of 7 IMPs, but only seven tricks in notrump (lose 6 IMPs for bidding game). If you are courageous enough to double 2♡, good defense will net you 300 (5 IMPs).

Deal 19

Dealer South, Both Vul.
N–S Datum +130

```
              ♠ 10 7 6
              ♡ K J 10 7
              ◇ J 2
              ♣ A K 6 5
            ┌─────────┐
            │    N    │
            │ W     E │
            │    S    │
            └─────────┘
              ♠ 8 4 2
              ♡ A 9
              ◇ A K Q 8 7 6 4
              ♣ 8
```

Deal 19 proved to be very difficult. Only two of eight pairs reached the proper spot, 3NT. Spades were 4-3 so nine tricks were easy. Both Levy-Mari and Martens-Szymanowski bid 1◇-1♡, 2◇-3NT. I'm not overly impressed, since if you switch South's black suits, North would be in a silly 3NT, cold for five or six diamonds.

How should North–South accurately bid these hands? After 1◇-1♡, 3◇ what should North do? At several tables he chose 3♠ and now how was poor South supposed to bid 3NT with a club stopper consisting of the singleton 8? Some Norths tried 4◇ on their second turn, also leading to the unsuccessful 5◇ game. Maybe this hand is just too tough.

Meckwell sat East-West, but I asked them how they would have bid this hand had they held it. Their answer was as simple as could be; they open a Gambling 3NT with the South hand (most experts would consider it too strong for such a preempt). They say they've had great success with this treatment, but it seems strange to me. They would have won 10 IMPs on this occasion, so who am I to argue?

Dealer West, N–S Vul.
N–S Datum +250

    ♠ K 9 7 6
    ♡ A Q J
    ◇ A 4 3
    ♣ Q 5 3

```
      N
   W     E
      S
```

    ♠ A 10
    ♡ K 10 8 4
    ◇ K 9 8 6 5 2
    ♣ 7

On Deal 20 we won a battle but lost the war. We were on VuGraph against Chagas–Branco, playing for first place, and bid as follows:

LARRY	DAVID
NORTH	SOUTH
1NT	2♣
2♠	3◇[1]
3♡	3♠
4◇	5◇

1. Natural, game–forcing.

Perhaps David was worth more than his final 5◇, because we'd have a great slam if I had the same hand with a fourth diamond. As it was, we had avoided the doomed 3NT (reached by two pairs), but what about the diamond slam?

Fortunately diamonds were 3–1, thus the datum was only 250. Winning 8 IMPs for 600 was nice, but we had been killed (on somewhat random game swings) on the three previous boards and dropped from having a chance of winning the event all the way down to sixth place.

It was not all bad news, since the top six pairs get an automatic invitation to next year's event; that means you can move on to Chapter 4!

Summary

Final standings

The top eight finishers were:

Chagas–Branco	(Brazil)	+121
Buratti–Lanzarotti	(Italy)	+90
Martens–Szymanowski	(Poland)	+80
Lauria–Versace	(Italy)	+50
Ming–Wang	(China)	+47
Berkowitz–Cohen	(USA)	+46
Lasut–Manoppo	(Indonesia)	+27
Meckstroth–Rodwell	(USA)	+16

Rating guide

- **Minus 20 or more IMPs** — Need to work on your slam bidding.
- **0 to -20 IMPs** — Not bad. After all, you were bidding against datums achieved by the "Top 16."
- **0 to +20 IMPs** — Well done. Your bidding results were better than some of the participants in The Hague.
- **+20 or more IMPs** — Maybe you should be invited to next year's event.

Scoring table

North-South datums and vulnerabilities

1. +1640	V		**2.** +510	V
3. +370	NV		**4.** +830	NV
5. +140	V		**6.** +270	V
7. +210	V		**8.** +830	NV
9. +340	NV		**10.** +620	V
11. +460	NV		**12.** +930	NV
13. +910	V		**14.** +620	NV
15. +690	NV		**16.** +440	V
17. +30	NV		**18.** +120	NV
19. +130	V		**20.** +250	V

CAP GEMINI 1998

David Berkowitz and I were fortunate enough to be invited to our fifth straight tournament in The Hague in January 1998. As usual, the organization and hospitality were up to the exceptionally high Dutch standards. There's still no doubt that this is the most glamorous (and difficult) bridge tournament in the world. There were 16 pairs all playing simultaneous 10-board matches scored by IMPs against the field. Try bidding these hands on pages 162 and 170 with your favorite partner and then match your results against the datum scores achieved in Holland.

ZIA MAHMOOD

TONY FORRESTER

Deal 1

Dealer West, N-S Vul.
N-S Datum +180

West opens 2◊; East bids 3◊.

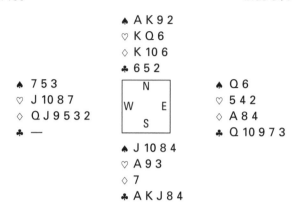

```
                    ♠ A K 9 2
                    ♡ K Q 6
                    ◊ K 10 6
                    ♣ 6 5 2
        ♠ 7 5 3         N           ♠ Q 6
        ♡ J 10 8 7   W     E        ♡ 5 4 2
        ◊ Q J 9 5 3 2      S        ◊ A 8 4
        ♣ —                         ♣ Q 10 9 7 3
                    ♠ J 10 8 4
                    ♡ A 9 3
                    ◊ 7
                    ♣ A K J 8 4
```

If you somehow managed to stop in 3NT or 4♠, you make your vulnerable game in comfort (for scoring purposes assume no overtricks, and take 9 and 10 IMPs respectively). If you got higher, you'll have to accept a minus score. True, you might make a higher-than-game contract in spades or notrump, but that's unlikely, as the real-life action in the Hague (and the low datum of +180) demonstrated. Several Norths played in 6♠ doubled and lost the first three tricks (♣3 ruffed, diamond over, club ruff) — so assume minus 500 and lose 12 IMPs if you reached 6♠. For 6NT, assume down three undoubled, which will cost you 8 IMPs. We reached 5♠ on the following auction:

WESTERHOF	BERKOWITZ	JANSEN	COHEN
WEST	NORTH	EAST	SOUTH
2♣[1]	dbl[2]	3◊[3]	4◊
pass	4♠	pass	5◊
pass	5♡	pass	5♠
all pass			

1. Many possibilities, usually a weak-two in diamonds.
2. 13-15 balanced or a very good hand.
3. Preemptive diamond raise.

Maybe I bid too much. East led the ◊A and shifted to a club, ruffed. David won the heart return, cashed a high spade, ruffed a diamond to dummy, and led the ♠J, on which West played low. Now what?

He agonized for a full five minutes and then finessed into the doubleton queen. Ugh! Down one. If you reached 5♠, assume minus 100 and lose 7 IMPs (they could also lead a club and beat you the easy way). Several declarers reached 4NT from North and received a low diamond lead to the jack. There were some winning lines available, but only one declarer succeeded (Norway's Tor Helness ducked the diamond lead, guessed correctly on the diamond continuation, and ended up with one diamond trick and three of everything else). Anyway, assume down one in 4NT (lose 7, but I'll make it up to you later).

This was a difficult deal, but it was a terrific demonstration of what aggressive preempting can do. At all five tables where West opened with a diamond preempt, North-South got too high. At the three tables where West passed, North opened 1NT and North-South stopped safely in 4♠ for +620 and a 10-IMP gain.

Deal 2

Dealer South, Neither Vul.
N-S Datum +450

```
              ♠ 10 9 8
              ♡ A K J 6
              ◇ A Q 7
              ♣ A 3 2
         ┌─────────────┐
         │      N      │
         │ W         E │
         │      S      │
         └─────────────┘
              ♠ A J 3
              ♡ Q 8 7 3
              ◇ K 5 4
              ♣ Q 6 5
```

There's a small piece of cheery news for anyone who reached five-of-a-major again: on this deal you'd survive with eleven tricks and +450. Similarly, eleven tricks were available in notrump. If you reached a small slam, take minus 50 and lose 11 IMPs. The field handled this hand beautifully, with nobody getting above game. Everybody opened the South hand, but the North players (wary of the aggressive-opening-bid style) took it real easy and let their partners out in 3NT or 4♡.

Deal 3

Dealer South, N-S Vul.
N-S Datum +910

*East overcalls 1♡ if
possible; West jump-
raises.*

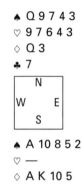

♠ Q 9 7 4 3
♡ 9 7 6 4 3
◇ Q 3
♣ 7

♠ A 10 8 5 2
♡ —
◇ A K 10 5
♣ A Q 9 5

This is not the deal that C.C. Wei dreamed of when he invented Precision. At the Standard American tables the auction went 1♠-4♠-6♠ for an easy 1430 (no bad breaks). None of the big-clubbers reached slam!

After South's strong club and North's minimum response it was easy for the favorable-vulnerability opponents to wreak havoc. We started 1♣-1◇ (negative) and East overcalled 1♡ on a four-bagger. I bid 1♠ and West jumped to 4♡. David bid 4♠ and that ended the auction with a 6-IMP loss. Both ladies' pairs (China's Wang-Sun and America's Letizia-Berkowitz) went +500 (and lost 9 IMPs) defending against 3♣ doubled after their opponents got busy over the big-club opening. Meckstroth-Rodwell also succumbed to the vigorous anti-Precision interference and stopped in 4♠ for +680.

Dealer North, E-W Vul.
N-S Datum +890

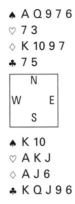

♠ A Q 9 7 6
♥ 7 3
♦ K 10 9 7
♣ 7 5

♠ K 10
♥ A K J
♦ A J 6
♣ K Q J 9 6

The cards were incredibly friendly, so assume that all small slams (except hearts!) will make. If you had to guess diamonds, assume you'd be successful. The best contract is 6NT, which has multiple chances. Against us Meckwell reached an inferior 6♠ (win 3 IMPs) after starting with a weak two-bid in spades by North.

The standards for an opening one-bid at this tournament were the lowest I've ever seen. England's Hackett brothers reached 6NT after Justin opened the North hand 1♠! At most tables South opened with a strong 2♣ (or a Precision 1♣) and in those cases 6NT was reached (win 3 IMPs).

Deal 5

Dealer East, N-S Vul.
N-S Datum +1700

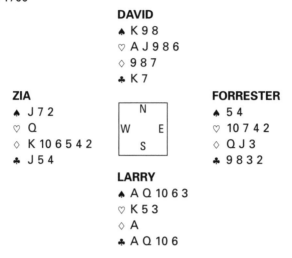

DAVID
♠ K 9 8
♡ A J 9 8 6
◊ 9 8 7
♣ K 7

ZIA
♠ J 7 2
♡ Q
◊ K 10 6 5 4 2
♣ J 5 4

FORRESTER
♠ 5 4
♡ 10 7 4 2
◊ Q J 3
♣ 9 8 3 2

LARRY
♠ A Q 10 6 3
♡ K 5 3
◊ A
♣ A Q 10 6

This one was a surprise. I opened the South hand with a strong club and Zia, West, bid 2♣ to show a one-suiter in either clubs or diamonds. David bid 2♡, natural and game-forcing, and Tony Forrester bid 3♣ (pass or correct). I raised hearts and eventually bid Roman Key Card Blackwood for hearts, settling in 6♡ when I found we were missing the ♡Q.

Tony led a club and David won the king in hand and laid down the ♡A. He was going to guard against ♡Q-10-x-x in Tony's hand. Zia's queen dropped and David led the ♡9, but went up with dummy's king (he didn't want to lose to Q-10 doubleton and 6-1 clubs!). Anyway, +1430 seemed good enough. Maybe a few pairs would miss this slam after starting with a 1♠ opening bid? Wrong! Nobody missed slam and three pairs reached 7♠. This contract was clearly anti-percentage, needing both major suits to behave. Both French pairs started 1♠-2♡, 3♣-3♠ and ended up +2210. Norway's Helgemo-Helness were helped along to the seven level by very active preemption from their opponents. For our satisfactory +1430 we sadly lost 7 IMPs.

Assume thirteen tricks in spades, but only twelve tricks in hearts (you'd misguess in seven), and score as follows: 6♡ lose 7 IMPs, 6♠ lose 6 IMPs, 7♡ lose 18 IMPs, 7♠ win 11 IMPs.

Dealer South, N-S Vul.
N-S Datum +1250

West bids 1♠ if possible.

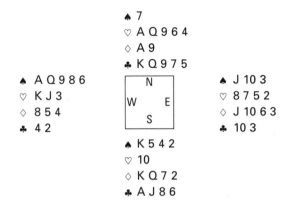

```
                    ♠ 7
                    ♡ A Q 9 6 4
                    ◇ A 9
                    ♣ K Q 9 7 5
    ♠ A Q 9 8 6        N          ♠ J 10 3
    ♡ K J 3       W         E     ♡ 8 7 5 2
    ◇ 8 5 4            S          ◇ J 10 6 3
    ♣ 4 2                         ♣ 10 3
                    ♠ K 5 4 2
                    ♡ 10
                    ◇ K Q 7 2
                    ♣ A J 8 6
```

The field had their bidding shoes on again, and once more the cards were friendly. Assume +1370 if you reached 6♣ (win 3 IMPs), but only eleven tricks in notrump. So lose 16 IMPs for bidding 6NT, and 11 IMPs for stopping in 3NT.

Perhaps France's Mari-Levy were tired after reaching 7♠ on the previous deal, since they reached only 5♣ against us on this one, and lost 12 IMPs:

	LEVY		**MARI**
WEST	NORTH	EAST	SOUTH
			1◇
1♠	2♡	pass	2NT
pass	3♣	pass	3◇
pass	3♠	pass	4♣
pass	5♣	all pass	

Given that Mari bid 4♣ (not 3NT), I think Levy's final 5♣ was an underbid. Still, a simple 4♣ by South over partner's 3♣ would have been better.

I suspect many readers will duplicate this auction until South's third call, when they will bid 4♣ instead of 3◇. Now North may Blackwood into slam. If your system is such that South can open 1♣, it makes the auction even easier and the slam is played from the better side. With North as declarer, after the ♠J lead from East and a spade continuation, declarer might have to finesse in hearts through the overcaller, and that is no sure thing.

Deal 7

Dealer East, N-S Vul.
N-S Datum +390

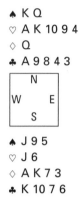

♠ K Q
♥ A K 10 9 4
♦ Q
♣ A 9 8 4 3

♠ J 9 5
♥ J 6
♦ A K 7 3
♣ K 10 7 6

Six clubs is worth reaching, since there are two ways to win. First, they might not find a spade lead, and second, you might bring in the clubs.

As you can tell from the low datum, some North-South pairs must have gone minus. Against us, Levy-Mari stopped in 5♣ making six, +620 for a 6-IMP gain. I led a diamond against five clubs from:

♠ 10 8 7 4 2   ♥ Q 2   ♦ 8 4 2   ♣ Q 5 2

so declarer pitched his spades and had an easy time making twelve tricks. But against six clubs, Forrester, Jansen, Lauria and Letizia all led spades (the auction was different). Three of the four declarers, faced with that unfortunate lead, misguessed the clubs for down one. Still, I think good bidding should be rewarded, so if you reached 6♣, assume +1370 and take 14 IMPs. Maybe this makes up for the tough scoring on Deal 1. If you reached any other reasonable game (3NT, 5♣, or even 4♥), assume eleven tricks and a positive swing.

Dealer West, Both Vul.
N-S Datum +1280

NORTH
♠ Q 4 3
♡ A 9
◇ A 7 4
♣ A Q 10 6 2

```
      N
  W       E
      S
```

SOUTH
♠ A K 7 6
♡ K Q 8 6 5 3
◇ 8
♣ J 5

We played Deals 6, 7 and 8 against Mari-Levy and they underbid all three of them. This time they stopped in 4♡ after this auction:

LEVY	MARI
NORTH	SOUTH
1NT	2♣
2◇	3♠[1]
3NT	4♡
pass	

1. Four spades and five-plus hearts, game-forcing.

What went wrong? They were yelling at each other in French, so I didn't understand the discussion. Both players had extras, but it's hard to say who I'd blame. In any event, hearts were 3-2 and the club finesse was wrong, so assume +1430 in 6♡ and win 4 IMPs. Six clubs is also a make for +1370 (win 3). However, spades split 4-2, so if you reached 6♠, 6NT, or 7♡, assume down one and chalk up minus 16 IMPs.

Deal 9

Dealer East, E-W Vul.
N-S Datum +380

```
              ♠ A K 5 4
              ♡ Q 8 7 6
              ◇ Q J 2
              ♣ 10 2
          ┌─────────┐
          │    N    │
          │ W     E │
          │    S    │
          └─────────┘
              ♠ 10
              ♡ A K 10 5
              ◇ A K 8 6 5
              ♣ K Q 4
```

This hand was the talk of the tournament. How do you play the heart suit in six hearts? This combination is well-known by experts from a defensive point of view. If East has ♡J-9-x-x in front of the ♡A-K-10-5, he must falsecard with the nine when declarer lays down his ace. If he fails to play the nine, declarer will have no choice but to play low to the queen on the next round, since there is only one 4-1 break he can pick up. By dropping the nine East gives him the option of playing for singleton nine and West for J-x-x-x. If the Q-8-7-6 is in dummy, declarer should lead the first round from dummy. Now RHO with J-9-x-x can't afford to falsecard with the nine because his partner might hold the singleton ten.

I was in 6♡ from the North hand and led a heart toward dummy's A-K-10-5 and, sure enough, Italy's Andrea Buratti, sitting East, played the dreaded nine! My table feel told me it was a singleton, so I continued with South's other high honor and was able to pick up Lanzarotti's J-4-3-2 for +980. Was this lucky? Was it good table feel? No, it was a bad play. At the local duplicate, by all means assume the nine is a singleton. But surely in this field everyone was capable of playing the nine from J-9-x-x, so in effect I went way against the 3-to-1 odds. The nine could have been from J-9-4-3, J-9-4-2, or J-9-3-2 — three possible holdings — and there was only one singleton nine. I should have assumed it was J-9-x-x and gone down.

Four out of seven declarers in 6♡ misguessed the suit. Denmark's Lars Blakset played the deal against Zia on VuGraph and he certainly didn't want to pay off to a falsecard. He looked at the nine long and hard, and decided to play it to be from J-9-x-x. Marcello Branco similarly misguessed against Meckwell. Later that night Rodwell told me that he had tossed his ♡9 onto the table with just the right body English. I felt that East had a singleton. Just not enough panache or style points on that play of the ♡9. So sue me for going against the odds.

How do we score this board? That's a toughie. I think the fairest thing is to assign a split ruling. We don't know how you'd guess, so take 0 IMPs for reaching 4♡ or 3NT (can't reward the wrong contract) but also 0 for 6♡ (you'd win or lose a bundle based on the heart guess). If, however, you reached the superior 6NT or 6◇, take +990 or +920 and either +12 IMPs or +11 IMPs (the ♣A was right in case you misguess the hearts).

Deal 10

Dealer East, Both Vul.
N-S Datum –80

```
              ♠ A K 5
              ♡ A K 6
              ◇ A 9 6 4
              ♣ 6 5 2
              ┌─────────┐
              │    N    │
              │ W     E │
              │    S    │
              └─────────┘
              ♠ 4
              ♡ J 8 2
              ◇ Q 7 5 3
              ♣ K J 9 7 4
```

This is the kind of hand where you know the field is going to be in the vulnerable game, even though it is an awful contract. I showed 17-18 balanced with the North hand, and David drove to 3NT. They led spades and I took the second round and decided my best chance was the ♣Q-10-x onside (that way the doubleton ace couldn't hold up and I could run the suit). I played a club to the nine and it won! I crossed to the diamond ace and led another club: ten, jack, show out. Oh, well. Plan B: I crossed to a heart and led a diamond toward the queen. Second hand played the 10 and... as I was thinking, West showed me the ◇KJ and I ended up down two. Obviously, we belonged in a partscore, but how should you stop?

The only pair to stay low was Brazil's Chagas-Branco, when Branco opened 1NT and played it there. Italy's Alfredo Versace was allowed to make 3NT when East mistakenly (for no good reason that I could see) grabbed the ♣A prematurely. Assume seven tricks in notrump, ten tricks in either minor. That will get you 5 IMPs for playing 1NT or a minor-suit partial. It will also cost you 5 IMPs for getting to 2NT, 7 IMPs for 3NT, and 5 IMPs for bidding game in a minor.

Dealer North, Neither Vul.
N-S Datum +90

```
                    ♠ K Q 10
                    ♡ J 8 7 3
                    ◊ 10 3 2
                    ♣ A Q J
               ┌─────────────┐
               │      N      │
               │ W        E  │
               │      S      │
               └─────────────┘
                    ♠ A J
                    ♡ A Q 10 6
                    ◊ A J 6 4
                    ♣ K 10 3
```

This is another exercise in trying to stay low. All the Norths opened the bidding and South found himself looking at 19 points and two tens. Everything was as wrong as could be, so ten tricks were the limit. Against us, the Hackett brothers reached 5♡, down one, and lost 4 IMPs. If you're wondering how to stop at the game level and win 9 IMPs, here are the successful auctions:

NORTH	SOUTH
RODWELL	MECKSTROTH
1◊	1♡
2♡	2♠
3NT	4♣
4♡	pass
PERRON	CHEMLA
1♣	1◊
1♡	1♠
1NT	3♡
3NT	4♣
4♡	pass
WESTRA	LEUFKENS
1♡	2NT
3NT	4♣
4♡	pass

Notice the diversity of bidding systems. Rodwell, playing Precision, opened 1◊. France's Michel Perron, playing standard, opened 1♣ and Holland's Berry Westra, playing four-card majors, opened 1♡. All the South players are apparently used to their partner's light opening bids.

Dealer South, E-W Vul.
N-S Datum +370

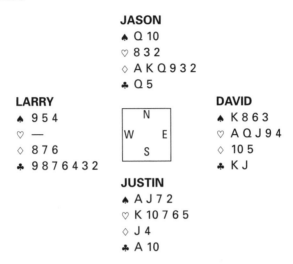

JASON
♠ Q 10
♡ 8 3 2
◇ A K Q 9 3 2
♣ Q 5

LARRY
♠ 9 5 4
♡ —
◇ 8 7 6
♣ 9 8 7 6 4 3 2

DAVID
♠ K 8 6 3
♡ A Q J 9 4
◇ 10 5
♣ K J

JUSTIN
♠ A J 7 2
♡ K 10 7 6 5
◇ J 4
♣ A 10

My partner doesn't like seeing this deal in print, but this is not its first public appearance. In fact, we played this deal on VuGraph against the Hackett twins (Justin and Jason) and their bidding was up to its usual aggressive (some might say youthfully optimistic) standard:

JASON	JUSTIN
NORTH	SOUTH
	1♡
2◇[1]	2♡
3♡	3♠
4◇	5♣
5◇	5♡
pass	

1. Game-forcing.

But the auction wasn't over. Now, tell the honest truth. Would you double 5♡ in the passout seat with David's hand?

♠ K 8 6 3　♡ A Q J 9 4　◇ 10 5　♣ K J

Should he worry they'll run to something they can make? Surely he can beat 6◇ (♡A and a ruff). So, he doubled and when this came around to Jason he indeed ran, but to 5NT. David doubled 5NT too. It was the macho thing to do, of course, but I will say he had lots of defense outside of hearts. He led the ♡Q, won in dummy. Declarer ran off six diamond tricks and there was no way to stop twelve tricks! There were six diamonds, three spades, one heart, one club, and a three-suit squeeze. We're lucky we got even one trick!

They have video cameras on all the players, and I heard they were laughing at me in the VuGraph room as I reached into the bidding box to look at the back of the 5NT card for the score. (It's minus 770 in case you're scoring at home.) If you're done snickering at us, it's time to calculate your own score. Assume ten tricks in hearts, eleven tricks in diamonds, and yes, twelve tricks in notrump. Any +990's out there to cover our minus 770?

Deal 13

Dealer East, Both Vul.
N-S Datum +530

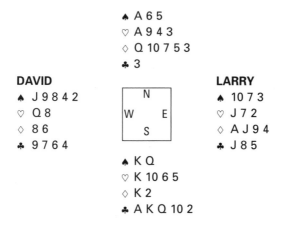

There seems to be a theme in this last bunch of deals, namely, stay low! Here, Roman Key Card in hearts with a follow-up ask for the trump queen should keep you out of 6♡. Against us, Poland's Martens-Szymanowski reached 6NT by South. David led a spade and declarer won and played the ◇K. Had I taken it, he could make the contract if he guessed to run the clubs and squeeze me in the red suits. However, I ducked smoothly and he continued diamonds for down one. Nobody succeeded in slam, so assume eleven tricks in hearts or notrump.

Score this deal as follows: 5♡, win 3 IMPs; 6♡, lose 12 IMPs; 5NT, win 4 IMPs; 6NT, lose 12 IMPs.

Dealer West, N-S Vul.
N-S Datum +1040

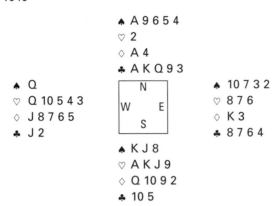

                    ♠ A 9 6 5 4
                    ♡ 2
                    ◇ A 4
                    ♣ A K Q 9 3
    ♠ Q   ♠ 10 7 3 2
    ♡ Q 10 5 4 3   N   ♡ 8 7 6
    ◇ J 8 7 6 5   W   E   ◇ K 3
    ♣ J 2   S   ♣ 8 7 6 4
                    ♠ K J 8
                    ♡ A K J 9
                    ◇ Q 10 9 2
                    ♣ 10 5

Again the Poles reached a slam against us, but this time they were successful, scoring 1430 in 6♠ to gain 9 IMPs. I led the ◇K against 6♠ and that made things real easy. Declarer laid down the ♠A and lost only a spade trick. However, the slam should make on any lead.

There was only one North-South minus score. Marcello Branco led the ♣J against 6NT and Holland's Jan Westerhof won in dummy and played a spade to the jack. When declarer regained the lead he laid down the ♠K and could no longer make the contract. Anyway, assume twelve tricks in clubs, spades, or notrump.

Score this deal as follows: 3NT or 5♠, lose 8 IMPs; 5♣, lose 9 IMPs; 6♣, win 8 IMPs; 6♠ or 6NT, win 9 IMPs.

Deal 15

Dealer South, Neither Vul.
N-S Datum +500

East bids 2♠, West raises.

```
              ♠ 10 8 2
              ♡ A
              ◊ Q J 5
              ♣ A Q 10 9 7 5
            ┌─────────────┐
            │      N      │
            │  W       E  │
            │      S      │
            └─────────────┘
              ♠ —
              ♡ K 8 5 2
              ◊ A 9 8 7 6 4 3
              ♣ 6 4
```

Chagas and Forrester both opened the South hand with a diamond preempt and thereafter could only reach game. Slam is almost a 75% proposition, since it requires little more than one of two finesses. In fact, East held the singleton ◊K and West held the ♣KJx, so everyone took all thirteen tricks in diamonds. The Chinese ladies defended four spades doubled and could collect only 300. Mari-Levy were still in their underbidding mode; they stopped in 4◊ on this auction:

RODWELL	MARI	MECKSTROTH	LEVY
West	North	East	South
			pass
pass	1♣	2♠	dbl
3♠	pass	pass	4◊
all pass			

I don't like the negative double. You expect your opponents to have a big spade fit and even if your side has a 4-4 heart fit, you don't rate to buy it in 4♡.

MARTENS	COHEN	SZYMANOWSKI	BERKOWITZ
West	North	East	South
			pass
pass	2♣	2♠	3◊
3♠	4◊	pass	4♠
pass	4NT[1]	pass	6◊
all pass			

1. Not Blackwood, but simply extras.

Plus 940 was a 10-IMP pickup, since Helgemo-Helness were the only other pair to reach a slam. Assume thirteen tricks in diamonds, eleven tricks in clubs, and eight tricks for East-West in spades.

84 · *Chapter Four*

Dealer North, Neither Vul.
N-S Datum +300

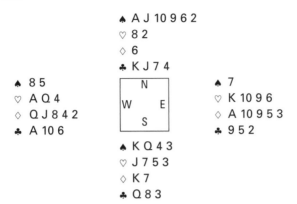

    ♠ A J 10 9 6 2
    ♡ 8 2
    ◇ 6
    ♣ K J 7 4

♠ 8 5
♡ A Q 4
◇ Q J 8 4 2
♣ A 10 6

♠ 7
♡ K 10 9 6
◇ A 10 9 5 3
♣ 9 5 2

    ♠ K Q 4 3
    ♡ J 7 5 3
    ◇ K 7
    ♣ Q 8 3

This deal caused much controversy. If you stopped in 3♠, good job, but why is the datum +300? At most tables North opened 1♠ and South drove to game.

BERKOWITZ	CHRISTIANSEN	COHEN	BLAKSET
WEST	NORTH	EAST	SOUTH
	1♠	pass	1NT
dbl	2♣	2♡	4♠
all pass			

I led a heart to the ace and David returned a trump. Declarer won and led a diamond up. You can see that I could win my ace and cash our four tricks. But I envisioned declarer with something like:

    ♠ A J 10 x x   ♡ x   ◇ Q x x   ♣ A x x x

(or the same hand with ♣ Kxxx). In that case, taking the ◇A would be fatal. After agonizing I ducked and went –420. In fact, this scenario was repeated at four tables! So why the controversy? This was one of the few deals that required a director's ruling and a committee. At one table the ♣2 was led against 4♠ and West took a long time at Trick 1 to insert the ten, which went to declarer's jack. When declarer led a diamond, East grabbed the ace and returned a club. The defense cashed out for down one. Declarer complained that East abused the information from the slow tempo at Trick 1 (he knew partner's slow ten must be from ace-ten; from K-10 the ten would be played without much thought). The Director ruled +420 for North-South and East-West appealed. The committee upheld the ruling and E-W did not take it well.

Just like Deal 9, this is one of those deals that can't be scored fairly as a bidding problem. There is no way to know how 4♠ would fare when you actually played it, but we're going to assign –8 IMPs for 4♠ and –4 IMPs for 3♠.

Deal 17

Dealer North, Both Vul.
N-S Datum +300

*If possible East opens
2♣ (natural, 11-15) and
West raises to 3♣.*

♠ Q 8 7
♡ 9 8 5
◇ A J 10 7 5
♣ 9 6

♠ A K J 9
♡ A J 10 7 4
◇ K Q 4
♣ Q

Without interference this would be an easy game to bid (perhaps with a mild try for slam along the way). At our table I opened the East hand 2♣ (11-15 HCP with six clubs) and South, Michel Perron, doubled. David jumped to four preemptive clubs, which was passed around back to Perron. He doubled again and Paul Chemla removed to 4◇. Perron did well to bid 4♡ over this and they scored +620 (hearts were 4-1 and repeated club leads plus careful declarer play resulted in ten tricks).

After a 3♣ raise by West, North might bid a direct 3◇; if he doesn't, I'd expect South to double again and North to remove to 3◇. At this point South has to make another move or the excellent game will be missed. Assume 4♡, 4♠ and 5◇ all make with no overtricks; take 8 IMPs for the major-suit games and 7 IMPs for 5◇. Heart, spade or diamond partscores lose you 4 IMPs.

Dealer South, N-S Vul.
N-S Datum +0

West opens 1♣.

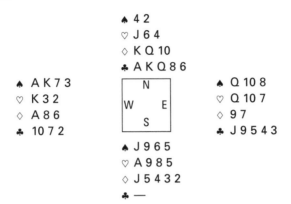

```
              ♠ 4 2
              ♡ J 6 4
              ◇ K Q 10
              ♣ A K Q 8 6
♠ A K 7 3       ┌─────────┐      ♠ Q 10 8
♡ K 3 2         │    N    │      ♡ Q 10 7
◇ A 8 6       W │         │ E    ◇ 9 7
♣ 10 7 2        │    S    │      ♣ J 9 5 4 3
                └─────────┘
              ♠ J 9 6 5
              ♡ A 9 8 5
              ◇ J 5 4 3 2
              ♣ —
```

After an opening 1♣ or 1◇ by West, most Norths would overcall 1NT and now it's up to South to make a winning decision after East's pass. At our table David had opened a Precision 1◇ on the West hand and Italy's Alfredo Versace over-called 1NT. Lorenzo Lauria bid Stayman and over the 2◇ response he retreated to an invitational 2NT. Versace passed, but they were already too high.

I led a club from the East seat to the ten and queen. Declarer played on dia-monds and David won the third round, severely damaging declarer's communi-cations. On that third diamond I threw the ♣J. David got the message and we played on majors for the rest of the hand. Declarer was never able to take his eight 'top' tricks; down one.

If you stopped in 1NT, assume +90. For 2◇ or 2♡ assume +110 (the play is tricky, but you deserve a plus score for avoiding 2NT or 3NT). For those Norths who passed 1♣ and then passed again after partner's balancing double, take –140 for 1♣ doubled making one.

Deal 19

Dealer South, Both Vul.
N-S Datum +640

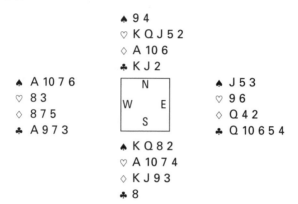

```
                    ♠ 9 4
                    ♡ K Q J 5 2
                    ◇ A 10 6
                    ♣ K J 2
    ♠ A 10 7 6          N          ♠ J 5 3
    ♡ 8 3                          ♡ 9 6
    ◇ 8 7 5       W         E      ◇ Q 4 2
    ♣ A 9 7 3         S            ♣ Q 10 6 5 4
                    ♠ K Q 8 2
                    ♡ A 10 7 4
                    ◇ K J 9 3
                    ♣ 8
```

The scoring of this set has benefited readers for the last few deals. Now it's makeup time. The ♠A was wrong, and if you reached the five-level, assume you would misguess the diamonds. Down one — sorry, lose 12 IMPs.

Meanwhile, if you stopped in 4♡, your reward is to guess correctly for no loss of IMPs. The best way to avoid the five-level is to diagnose the club wastage. We started 1◇-1♡, 3♡. In Standard, the South hand is worth a raise to 3♡ only if you play real light opening bids (in which case that 4-4-4-1 13-count looks like extras). In our Precision style, 3♡ was just about right, especially since we play it guarantees short clubs or spades. I asked with the North hand and found out that David had a stiff club.

Slam would be worthwhile opposite

♠ A x x   ♡ A x x x   ◇ K Q x x x   ♣ x

so I made one more try, but he signed off in 4♡. I guessed the ◇Q, but I know that if I was in five, it wouldn't have been as easy!

If you reached 3NT, you also go down (club lead, diamond misguess) and lose 12 IMPs.

Dealer East, Both Vul.
N-S Datum –150

East opens 3◊.

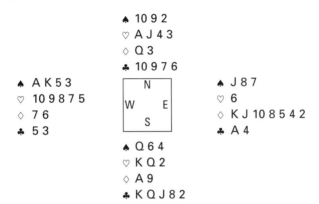

```
              ♠ 10 9 2
              ♡ A J 4 3
              ◊ Q 3
              ♣ 10 9 7 6
♠ A K 5 3          N          ♠ J 8 7
♡ 10 9 8 7 5   W       E      ♡ 6
◊ 7 6              S          ◊ K J 10 8 5 4 2
♣ 5 3                         ♣ A 4
              ♠ Q 6 4
              ♡ K Q 2
              ◊ A 9
              ♣ K Q J 8 2
```

That South collection is the classical headache hand. Do you overcall 3NT direct-ly over 3◊? I think not. But, if you double and partner bids the expected (dread-ed) three-of-a-major, now what? 3NT this time? Does that show more than a 3NT overcall, or is it suggesting alternative contracts (I prefer the latter treatment). Do you pass partner's three-of-a-major? Raise him to four? I like to assume part-ner has about 5-8 points on average and bid accordingly. In this example that doesn't help; it's a bit of a guess.

David, who announced that he was in his blue period (the deals were run-ning in a manner where staying low was the winning action), doubled and passed 3♡. I couldn't handle the 5-1 trump break and finished down one for a small IMP gain. Chagas-Branco and Chemla-Perron landed in the disastrous 3NT by South. They both won the second round of diamonds and played on clubs. The defense started running diamonds and then shifted to spades. On a really bad day declarer would be down eight (if West had ♠A-K-J-x-x)! Fortunately, the spades behaved, so 3NT was down only five.

If you somehow (I don't know how) reached 3NT by North, assume they wouldn't find the spade lead and diamond back, so +630 (win 13 IMPs)! Assume eight tricks in hearts (win 2 in 3♡, lose 2 in 4♡), nine tricks in clubs (lose 2 in 4♣, lose 4 in 5♣) and, as you've seen, four tricks if South declares notrump (lose 8 for 3NT by South).

Summary

There were two themes running throughout this set of deals. One, if you tend to open light, your partner better be aware of it and keep you low. Two, the level of play at this particular tournament was well below what you'd expect. I was particularly dissatisfied with our performance; we never seem to play well in Europe. In fact, this Cap Gemini Tournament has always proved difficult for Americans (Meckwell are 0 for 8); maybe it's something about the jetlag. Or maybe the sun was in our eyes?

Final standings

The top ten pairs were:

Zia-Forrester	(USA-UK)	+107
Buratti-Lanzarotti	(Italy)	+86
Helness-Helgemo	(Norway)	+65
Hackett-Hackett	(UK)	+48
Chagas-Branco	(Brazil)	+46
Berkowitz-Cohen	(USA)	+33
Meckstroth-Rodwell	(USA)	+27
Jansen-Westerhof	(Netherlands)	+3
Martens-Szymanowski	(Poland)	+0
Chemla-Perron	(France)	-6

Rating guide

Collect Your Prize

- **Below -20 IMPs**   You didn't really expect one, did you?
- **-20 to 0 IMPs**   Sorry, almost good enough
- **0 to +20 IMPs**   A tulip
- **Above +20 IMPs**   A windmill

Scoring table

North-South datums and vulnerabilities

1. +180	V		**2.** +450	NV	
3. +910	V		**4.** +890	NV	
5. +1700	V		**6.** +1250	V	
7. +390	V		**8.** +1280	V	
9. +380	NV		**10.** -80	V	
11. +90	NV		**12.** +370	NV	
13. +530	V		**14.** +1040	V	
15. +500	NV		**16.** +300	NV	
17. +300	V		**18.** 0	V	
19. +640	V		**20.** -150	V	

POLITIKEN 1998

The second running of the Politiken Pairs took place in November 1998 in Copenhagen, Denmark. There were good playing conditions with ample room for kibitzers, and there was also a live VuGraph presentation. Only sixteen pairs were invited to this special event, but thirteen different countries were represented: Canada, China, Denmark, Germany, Great Britain, Holland, Iceland, India, Norway, Pakistan, Poland, Sweden and the United States.

The winners, with an incredible total (see page 112), were Norway's Geir Helgemo and Poland's Krzysztof (great scrabble score) Martens. The defending champions, Zia Mahmood and Peter Weichsel, came in sixteenth. If two players of that caliber can come in last, it must mean that the field was pretty good. This time I will focus on the results David Berkowitz and I achieved (and trust me, it will be embarrassing at times), with a sprinkling of my opinions. Perhaps you will ignore my advice when you see some of our auctions. No laughing permitted. Try bidding the hands yourself first — they on pages 163 and 171.

GEIR HELGEMO

KRZYSZTOF MARTENS

Deal 1

Dealer West, Both Vul.
N–S Datum +480

East bids 1♠.

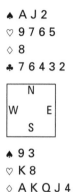

♠ A J 2
♡ 9 7 6 5
◇ 8
♣ 7 6 4 3 2

♠ 9 3
♡ K 8
◇ A K Q J 4
♣ A Q J 8

Either 3NT or 5♣ makes with ease on these cards. In fact, you'd score 1370 and win 14 IMPs if you reached 6♣ (singleton ♣K onside, ♡A onside, diamonds 4–3). Take 620 for 5♣, or 630 for 3NT (win 4 for either contract).

After East opens 1♠, I think it's quite reasonable to bid 3♠ with the South hand (the most common use for this bid is to ask partner to bid 3NT with spades stopped). All South really needs to have play for 3NT is something like:

♠ Q J x   ♡ x x x x   ◇ x x x   ♣ 10 x x

and in fact many similar hands will give him play for nine tricks.

David doubled the 1♠ opening bid (he never does what I would have done) and I had a decision to make. In retrospect, I like 2♣ from the North hand, which gives more room to investigate. At the table I tried 2♡ (thinking that the major is what partner most likely wants to hear) and David probably should have cue-bid 2♠, but he bid a very heavy and nonforcing 3◇. I passed, thinking, 'If all he needed was a spade stopper, he could have bid 3♠ the first time.' Wrong again — plus 130, but a loss of only 8 IMPs, since two of the other seven pairs also played in a partscore.

Dealer East, Both Vul.
N–S Datum +140

$\spadesuit$ A 5
$\heartsuit$ A K
$\diamond$ K Q 3
$\clubsuit$ A K 6 5 3 2

```
      N
  W       E
      S
```

$\spadesuit$ 8 4 2
$\heartsuit$ Q J 8 7 6 4
$\diamond$ 6 5 2
$\clubsuit$ J

If South opens with a heart preempt (very aggressive, in my opinion, for second seat vulnerable), no doubt 6$\heartsuit$ will be reached. Assume a spade lead and down one, and deduct 6 IMPs from your score. You can also assume a spade lead against the inferior game contracts of 3NT and 5$\clubsuit$, leading to down two and a loss of 8 IMPs.

Against us China's Fu Zhong opened 2NT with the big hand (I think he's way too strong for that) and Wang Xiao Jing placed the contract in four hearts. For –650 we lost a surprising 11 IMPs.

Deal 3

Dealer East, N–S Vul.
N–S Datum: +320

West bids 1♡ if possible
and East raises.

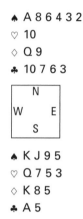

♠ A 8 6 4 3 2
♡ 10
♢ Q 9
♣ 10 7 6 3

♠ K J 9 5
♡ Q 7 5 3
♢ K 8 5
♣ A 5

Some Souths opened 1♡ (four-card majors) and that kept the opponents silent. Over one of either red suit I don't see why North can't bid 1♠, South 2♠, and then North 4♠. (Am I being over-influenced by the perfect layout?) This is especially true if South's opening bid is 1♢; in that case, North has a terrific fit.

Anyway, only three pairs bid the laydown spade game, so we gained 4 IMPs when our opponents started with a 12–14 notrump and landed in only 3♠. Peter Weichsel and Zia Mahmood (the defending champions) were permitted to play in (and make) four hearts the other way! Take 7 IMPs if you got to four spades.

Dealer West, Both Vul.
N–S Datum +170

West opens 2♡ (0-11, at least nine cards in the majors).

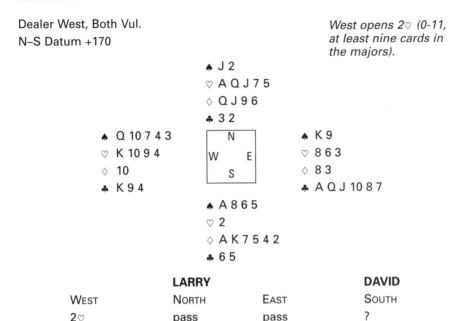

```
                    ♠ J 2
                    ♡ A Q J 7 5
                    ◊ Q J 9 6
                    ♣ 3 2
    ♠ Q 10 7 4 3        N        ♠ K 9
    ♡ K 10 9 4      W       E    ♡ 8 6 3
    ◊ 10                S        ◊ 8 3
    ♣ K 9 4                      ♣ A Q J 10 8 7
                    ♠ A 8 6 5
                    ♡ 2
                    ◊ A K 7 5 4 2
                    ♣ 6 5
```

	LARRY		**DAVID**
WEST	NORTH	EAST	SOUTH
2♡	pass	pass	?

If you play in Europe, you'd better be prepared for lots of funny gadgets. Unlike ACBL-land, most other parts of the world have an anything goes (within reason) attitude. It only seems right to present you with one of these gadgets (over the course of four days we faced about seven or eight auctions that started with a funny two-bid).

On this one, we hit the jackpot. I passed the 2♡ opening around to David and he judged quite well to double with the South hand. I think I would have balanced with 3◊ with his hand, over which we might have reached 3NT, down two, off the first six club tricks (lose 9 IMPs). Over his double, I happily passed, and we scored an easy 800 for down three, picking up a useful 12 IMPs. Assume a club lead against a diamond contract, which holds it to ten tricks, so lose 1 IMP for a diamond partial, and lose 7 for climbing all the way to five diamonds.

Deal 5

Dealer West, N–S Vul.
N–S Datum +870

East overcalls 1♠ if possible; West raises to 5♠.

```
                    ♠ Q 4
                    ♡ A 8 6 3
                    ◇ A Q 4 3
                    ♣ K Q 9
                  ┌─────────┐
                  │    N    │
                  │ W     E │
                  │    S    │
                  └─────────┘
                    ♠ 7
                    ♡ K Q 10 9 7 5 2
                    ◇ 10
                    ♣ A 10 5 3
```

If you were fortunate enough to be playing strong notrumps, the opponents remained silent on this deal. If the auction starts 1NT–2◇ (transfer), 2♡–3♣, North will have quite a good hand for his opening notrump, and will only have to find out that spades are controlled to push on to slam.

We had to start with a big club, which let the opponents into the auction in a big way. East overcalled 1♠ on a 5-2-4-2 nine-count and over David's game-forcing 2♡, West the pest jumped to 5♠. At this point I think I used poor judgment. We play a Meckwell convention here, 'pass–double inversion'. Double is an invitation to 6♡ and pass asks partner to double (after which you can pass for penalties or pull to show various hand-types). I didn't think I had too much extra (for a strong club) so I elected to pass and defend 5♠ doubled, down 300 (we took two clubs, a diamond, and a diamond ruff), and lost 11 IMPs.

In retrospect, I think I was worth an invitation due to my good hearts and decent controls. I can't blame David; from his point of view I could have had some hand with a singleton heart. If you reached 6♡, assume they'd let you play it there, and take 1430 for a pickup of 11 IMPs.

Dealer West, Both Vul.
N–S Datum +500

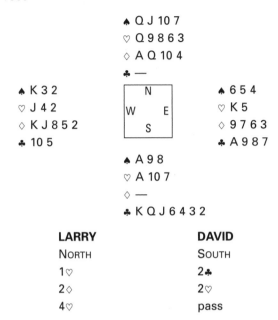

♠ Q J 10 7
♡ Q 9 8 6 3
◇ A Q 10 4
♣ —

♠ K 3 2
♡ J 4 2
◇ K J 8 5 2
♣ 10 5

♠ 6 5 4
♡ K 5
◇ 9 7 6 3
♣ A 9 8 7

♠ A 9 8
♡ A 10 7
◇ —
♣ K Q J 6 4 3 2

LARRY	DAVID
NORTH	SOUTH
1♡	2♣
2◇	2♡
4♡	pass

If North opens with Flannery 2◇, South should be able to find out about the mis-fitting minor–suit distribution and put on the brakes in time to stop in 4♡. As you can see, 5♣ would fail, since clubs were 4-2 and the spade finesse was wrong; lose 12 IMPs for being there. If you reached 4♡, assume you'd choose a good line of play and score 620 (one declarer failed in 4♡) for a win of 3 IMPs. For any slam, assume down two and lose 12 IMPs.

I opened the North hand 1♡ and David bid 2♣, game forcing. Even though we play that a 2♠ rebid doesn't guarantee extras, I chose the more flexible 2◇. Not only would this allow more room, but it was the suit that contained more than half my high–card strength. David forced with 2♡ and, instead of 'pattern-ing out', I jumped to 4♡. We play fast arrival, so this showed a very weak hand. I had awful trumps, an awful club fit, and no control in the unbid suit. David decided it was a misfit and correctly passed, allowing us to go plus and gain 3 IMPs.

Some experts think that light three–suited hands make for poor opening bids, because of the difficulty in describing the hand without overstating the val-ues. A good way to stop in 4♡ is for North to pass initially. South opens 1♣ (play-ing Standard) and then rebids 3♣. North is not wild about slam after this start.

Deal 7

Dealer East, Both Vul.
N–S Datum +390

East opens 1◊; West bids 2◊.

    ♠ A K Q
    ♡ 7 6
    ◊ Q 5 4
    ♣ J 8 7 6 4

```
      N
  W       E
      S
```

    ♠ 9 6 3
    ♡ J 9 8 2
    ◊ K 2
    ♣ A K Q 2

This is a tough one. It's a perfect fit, and you can take nine tricks in notrump, ten tricks in clubs. It's difficult for North to bid 3NT on his own, because his diamond stopper looks so tenuous. True, on a bad day the defense might beat you in 3NT by taking four heart tricks, but you rate to get a diamond lead.

Against us Zia (South) doubled David's limited 1◊, and Weichsel tried a responsive double after my raise to 2◊. Now, Zia bid 2♡ and Peter bid only 2NT and played there for +150 and a loss of 6 IMPs.

Score this one as follows: win 5 IMPs for 3NT, lose 7 IMPs for a club partscore, and lose 11 IMPs if you got all the way to five clubs.

Dealer East, Both Vul.
N–S Datum +500

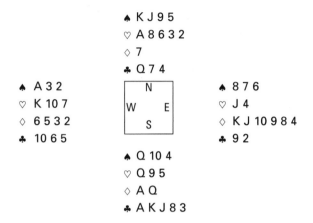

```
              ♠ K J 9 5
              ♡ A 8 6 3 2
              ◇ 7
              ♣ Q 7 4
  ♠ A 3 2        N          ♠ 8 7 6
  ♡ K 10 7    W     E       ♡ J 4
  ◇ 6 5 3 2      S          ◇ K J 10 9 8 4
  ♣ 10 6 5                  ♣ 9 2
              ♠ Q 10 4
              ♡ Q 9 5
              ◇ A Q
              ♣ A K J 8 3
```

Most auctions start 1♣ by South, 1♡ by North, 2NT by South. Over this, North certainly must entertain the thought of a slam in any of three suits (unless 2NT denies four spades). With the actual South hand, if the ♡Q were the king, 6♣ would be virtually laydown. We got into trouble evaluating the potential of these hands. David opened the South hand a strong club and I showed a game force with at least a five–card heart suit. Several cuebids later David launched Roman Key Card but then came to a screeching halt in 5♡ when we were off two key-cards.

If I had been equipped with X–ray vision, I could have taken eleven tricks (I had to take an intra–finesse — heart to the nine and then lead the queen, to pin East's doubleton jack). Being a mere mortal, I played ♡A and a heart, and the jack appeared from East. I tortured myself for a minute or two, trying to guess if West had a doubleton heart king, but I was wasting my time. Down one and an expensive loss of 12 IMPs, since only one other pair got too high. Assume ten tricks in hearts, eleven in notrump or clubs.

Score yourself as follows: four hearts, win 3 IMPs; 3NT, win 4 IMPs; five clubs, win 3 IMPs; any higher, lose 12 IMPs.

Deal 9

Dealer West, Neither Vul.
N–S Datum +340

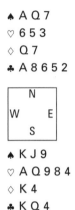

♠ A Q 7
♡ 6 5 3
◊ Q 7
♣ A 8 6 5 2

♠ K J 9
♡ A Q 9 8 4
◊ K 4
♣ K Q 4

After you read Deal 8, and now this one, you'll never want David and me as your teammates. I opened the North hand with a 10-12 notrump, and David bid game-forcing Stayman and then showed five hearts (over my 3♣ response). I bid 3♡ and then cuebid 4♣ over his 3NT. (I loved my two aces and three trumps; perhaps I should have hated the fact that I had no hearts above the six-spot). He envisioned king-third of hearts, ace-fifth of clubs, and another ace — that would give us great play for six hearts.

Déjà vu. He bid Roman Key Card again, stopped in 5♡ again, and again we got punished when there were two trumps losers — down one. These weren't our best two auctions ever, but when things are going right you survive and take eleven tricks anyway. Maybe Americans just bid too much — on both Deal 8 and Deal 9 Weichsel and Zia were the only other pair to get to the five-level.

Assume ten tricks in notrump or hearts, and score as follows: six-level contracts, lose 11 IMPs; five-level contracts, lose 10 IMPs; four notrump, win 7 IMPs; four hearts, win 6 IMPs.

Dealer North, Both Vul.
N–S Datum: +1050

```
              ♠ A 9 5
              ♡ A K J
              ◇ J 6 5 2
              ♣ K 8 3
            ┌─────────┐
            │    N    │
            │ W     E │
            │    S    │
            └─────────┘
              ♠ K Q J 8 6 4
              ♡ Q 4 2
              ◇ K Q 8 3
              ♣ —
```

Well, we can't lose them all. We were one of four pairs to reach this excellent slam. Diamonds were 3-2 so 6♠ or 6◇ were easy makes. I started with a 14–16 notrump and David transferred to spades. Next he bid 3◇, natural, and I bid 3♠, which showed a good hand (with a bad hand I'd have jumped to 4♠). Now, David took a chance that I had a heart control (it's a pretty good percentage bet) and jumped to 5♣, Exclusion Key Card Blackwood. I showed two keycards outside of clubs and David bid 6♠ for +1430 and a useful 9-IMP gain.

David was a bit fortunate that my minor-suit jack was in diamonds, as opposed to clubs. On the other hand, I did have a wasted ♡J and ♣K. If I had four small diamonds, the slam would be less than 50%, and the way our luck was going on Deals 8 and 9, the trend would have been for the ◇A to be wrong on Deal 10.

If you got to six diamonds, which is an inferior contract, you still get 8 IMPs. Five diamonds loses you 10 IMPs, and four spades costs you 9 IMPs.

Deal 11

Dealer East, N–S Vul.
N–S Datum +280

East opens 3♠, West bids 4♠.

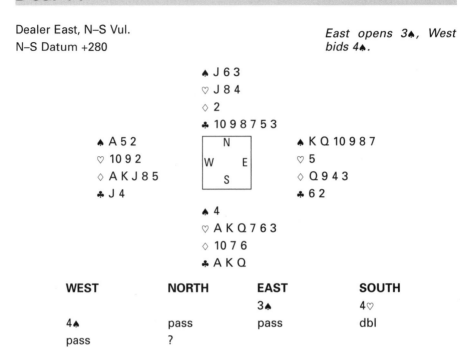

	♠ J 6 3	
	♡ J 8 4	
	◇ 2	
	♣ 10 9 8 7 5 3	
♠ A 5 2		♠ K Q 10 9 8 7
♡ 10 9 2		♡ 5
◇ A K J 8 5		◇ Q 9 4 3
♣ J 4		♣ 6 2
	♠ 4	
	♡ A K Q 7 6 3	
	◇ 10 7 6	
	♣ A K Q	

WEST	NORTH	EAST	SOUTH
		3♠	4♡
4♠	pass	pass	dbl
pass	?		

This deal involved more luck than any other in the tournament. At most tables the auction started as shown above. Six Norths pulled to 5♡ and got doubled, and four pairs scored 850. The other two were one down. (For the purposes of scoring, we'll assume you'd take eleven tricks after the ◇K lead and a trump shift. You could go down if you chose to play for clubs 3-1 and hearts 2-2 by drawing a second round of trumps. The successful line of ruffing two diamonds requires two club entries, unless West shifts to spades at trick two, which he might do to save the 200-point overtrick. In any event, we'll give you 11 IMPs for bidding 5♡.)

The other two Norths elected to defend 4♠ doubled, which was unbeatable, –590 and 13 IMPs down the drain. Notice what a cruel and random game this can be. Switch South's minors and the two Norths who passed 4♠ doubled would be the winners. How could they know?

Dealer East, N–S Vul.
N–S Datum –180

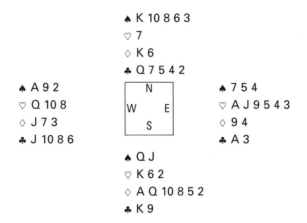

```
              ♠ K 10 8 6 3
              ♡ 7
              ◊ K 6
              ♣ Q 7 5 4 2
♠ A 9 2          N          ♠ 7 5 4
♡ Q 10 8     W       E      ♡ A J 9 5 4 3
◊ J 7 3          S          ◊ 9 4
♣ J 10 8 6                  ♣ A 3
              ♠ Q J
              ♡ K 6 2
              ◊ A Q 10 8 5 2
              ♣ K 9
```

The only makable game is 4♠. David overcalled East's 2♡ opening with 2NT on the South hand and I transferred to spades and then bid 3NT. David passed, they led hearts and we were down three. (They took five heart tricks and two aces after the heart lead was ducked to the king; David tried to sneak through a spade — a reasonable ploy.) Perhaps I should have bid 3♣ and then 3♠ to suggest a less balanced hand. I don't blame David for passing 3NT, but it was possible to consider playing in a 5–2 spade fit.

If David had overcalled 3◊ instead of 2NT, it's not clear what would have happened. I'd probably have bid 3♠ and we still might have ended up in 3NT. We had lots of company; six of eight pairs played in the doomed notrump game, and only one pair went plus with our cards!

Assume seven tricks in notrump, ten in diamonds, and ten tricks in spades, so the scoring is as follows: 2NT, win 2 IMPs; 3◊, win 7 IMPs; 3♠, win 8 IMPs; 3NT, lose 1 IMP; 4◊, win 2 IMPs; 4♠, win 10 IMPs; 5◊, win 2 IMPs.

Deal 13

Dealer North, Neither Vul.
N–S Datum +690

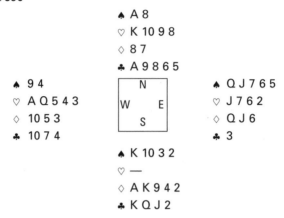

```
              ♠ A 8
              ♡ K 10 9 8
              ◇ 8 7
              ♣ A 9 8 6 5
  ♠ 9 4          N        ♠ Q J 7 6 5
  ♡ A Q 5 4 3  W   E      ♡ J 7 6 2
  ◇ 10 5 3       S        ◇ Q J 6
  ♣ 10 7 4                ♣ 3
              ♠ K 10 3 2
              ♡ —
              ◇ A K 9 4 2
              ♣ K Q J 2
```

Finally, a good board for us. I opened a 10–12 notrump on the North hand and David bid game-forcing Stayman. I bid 2♡ and David made a very good decision. Had he bid 3◇, we might have lost the clubs, but he bid a forcing 2NT, allowing me to bid 3♣. From there we ended up in 6♣, which made in comfort. Seven clubs is a reasonable contract, but the breaks were just awkward enough to make it difficult to handle.

If you reached 7♣, assume you'd make it half the time and go down half the time, for an average result of +695 (1440–50 divided by 2) and no swing. For other club contracts assume twelve tricks (win 6 IMPs for 6♣, lose 7 IMPs for 5♣). Also assume eleven tricks in diamonds (lose 7 IMPs for 5◇) and ten tricks in notrump (lose 6 IMPs for 3NT). Only half the field bid and made a slam.

Dealer South, E–W Vul.
N–S Datum –50

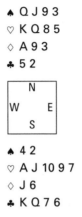

       ♠ Q J 9 3
       ♡ K Q 8 5
       ◇ A 9 3
       ♣ 5 2

       ♠ 4 2
       ♡ A J 10 9 7
       ◇ J 6
       ♣ K Q 7 6

This one is to keep proponents of sound opening bids happy. The very modern field routinely opened the South hand 1♡ and drove the North hand to the no-play 4♡. To me, this is just one of those things. In fact, all eight tables played in four hearts. Of course, even if you pass as South, North will open in third, and once hearts are mentioned, you will probably get to game pretty quickly anyhow.

So no swing if you reached four hearts, but take 5 IMPs if you somehow managed to avoid getting that high.

Deal 15

Dealer East, Neither Vul.
N–S Datum +710

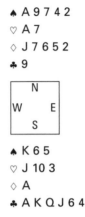

♠ A 9 7 4 2
♡ A 7
◇ J 7 6 5 2
♣ 9

♠ K 6 5
♡ J 10 3
◇ A
♣ A K Q J 6 4

This one is a bit tricky. Six spades is worth being in, since it requires little more than a 3-2 spade break (a 68% chance). We explored slam (after a strong club opener) and stopped in 4♠. Perhaps it's just as well, as there is a good chance that in many auctions the South hand will toy around with spades, but then place the final contract into the solidity of that club suit, namely in six clubs. That contract would fail on the likely heart lead.

Only one pair reached 6♣ (down one for a loss of 13 IMPs). The rest of the field was roughly split between game and slam in spades. Trumps were indeed 3-2, so that's 480 (lose 6 IMPs) or 980 (win 7 IMPs) for you spade bidders. Assume ten tricks in the unlikely event you reached 3NT, and award yourself a loss of 7 IMPs. Assume a heart lead against a club contract and only eleven tricks on best play, so lose 7 IMPs also for five clubs.

Dealer North, E–W Vul.
N–S Datum +420

```
                    ♠ Q 9 6 2
                    ♡ K Q J 10 4 2
                    ◇ A K 8
                    ♣ —
                 ┌─────────┐
                 │    N    │
                 │ W     E │
                 │    S    │
                 └─────────┘
                    ♠ A J 10
                    ♡ 9 6
                    ◇ 7 4 3 2
                    ♣ Q 5 4 2
```

This one was inserted into this chapter as a breather (or maybe a confidence builder). It's probably the easiest deal of the twenty. Seven of the eight pairs reached 4♡ and took ten tricks (the ♠K was offside). I believe the auction should go 1♡–1NT, 2♠ – 3♠, 4♡ – pass. Assume ten tricks in hearts, nine tricks in spades, and seven tricks in notrump.

Score yourself as follows: 4♡, no swing; 4♠, lose 10 IMPs; heart partials, lose 6 IMPs; spade partials, lose 7 IMPs; 3NT, lose 11 IMPs; 2NT, lose 10 IMPs; 1NT, lose 8 IMPs.

Deal 17

Dealer West, N–S Vul.
N–S Datum +1380

West opens 3◊.

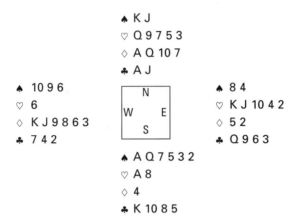

```
                    ♠ K J
                    ♡ Q 9 7 5 3
                    ◇ A Q 10 7
                    ♣ A J
      ♠ 10 9 6         N          ♠ 8 4
      ♡ 6         W         E      ♡ K J 10 4 2
      ◇ K J 9 8 6 3      S         ◇ 5 2
      ♣ 7 4 2                      ♣ Q 9 6 3
                    ♠ A Q 7 5 3 2
                    ♡ A 8
                    ◇ 4
                    ♣ K 10 8 5
```

To score yourselves, assume that all lines of play lead to twelve tricks in spades or notrump. Most Norths overcalled West's diamond preempt with 3NT and all the Souths then drove to a small slam and won 2 IMPs (actually, our South only invited with 5♠, but North accepted). The only accident occurred when Peter Weichsel overcalled 3NT and Zia transferred to 4♠ and then bid 4NT. He intended it as Blackwood, but Peter took it as quantitative and passed.

The bidding system after a 3NT overcall is rarely discussed. Another accident occurred to Matthew and Pamela Granovetter, who bid these hands for practice, much like you are doing. They landed in 6♣ after South transferred to spades, cuebid diamonds and then offered clubs as a contract at the six-level. North (Matthew) passed this. (Actually, 6♣ makes after a heart lead: diamond finesse, club finesse, leave the last trump out and run the spades!)

At one table, North passed the 3◊ opening bid and South reopened with a double. The declarer could take only three tricks! So if you defended 3◊ doubled, assume down six, +1400 and a 1–IMP gain.

Dealer West, Neither Vul.
N–S Datum +400

East bids spades; West raises to 3♠ if possible (weak if a jump).

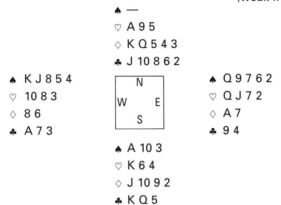

```
                    ♠ —
                    ♡ A 9 5
                    ◇ K Q 5 4 3
                    ♣ J 10 8 6 2
  ♠ K J 8 5 4                        ♠ Q 9 7 6 2
  ♡ 10 8 3          N                ♡ Q J 7 2
  ◇ 8 6         W       E            ◇ A 7
  ♣ A 7 3           S                ♣ 9 4
                    ♠ A 10 3
                    ♡ K 6 4
                    ◇ J 10 9 2
                    ♣ K Q 5
```

	LARRY		**DAVID**
WEST	NORTH	EAST	SOUTH
pass	1◇	1♠	3♠[1]
dbl	4♣	pass	4◇
pass	5◇	all pass	

1. See text for explanation.

I'd rate this the second easiest of this chapter's twenty deals. For one of the few times of the week, we were successful in a five-level contract. David's 3♠ was a 3NT bid (13-15), but a request to play it from the other side. No, I don't play them better than David; we just think it's good to put the overcaller on lead. West's double of 3♠ asked for a spade lead, but I rejected the notrump idea and bid my second suit.

There were no bad breaks, so assume eleven tricks in either minor. An unlikely defense would beat 5◇ (East must lead a club, ducked, and then he wins the trump ace and plays a club to his partner for a ruff). Five clubs could not be defeated. Assume down two in 3NT. All eight tables scored eleven tricks in five-of-a-minor.

Minor partscores cost you 6 IMPs, 3NT costs you 11 IMPs, and bidding your minor-suit game lets you escape unscathed to the next problem.

Deal 19

Dealer East, N–S Vul.
N–S Datum +250

East opens 3♠; West bids 4♠.

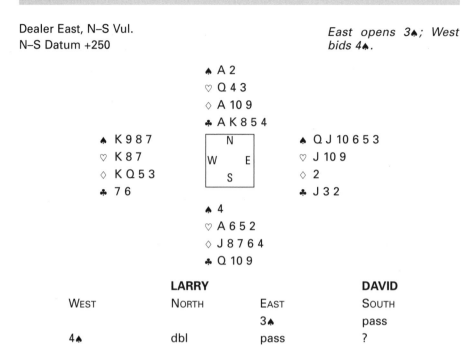

```
                    ♠ A 2
                    ♡ Q 4 3
                    ◇ A 10 9
                    ♣ A K 8 5 4
    ♠ K 9 8 7      ┌─────────┐      ♠ Q J 10 6 5 3
    ♡ K 8 7        │    N    │      ♡ J 10 9
    ◇ K Q 5 3      │ W     E │      ◇ 2
    ♣ 7 6          │    S    │      ♣ J 3 2
                   └─────────┘
                    ♠ 4
                    ♡ A 6 5 2
                    ◇ J 8 7 6 4
                    ♣ Q 10 9
```

	LARRY		**DAVID**
WEST	NORTH	EAST	SOUTH
		3♠	pass
4♠	dbl	pass	?

I don't like to pull this kind of double without extreme shape; I've found that a good rule of thumb is to pull when you have a singleton or void in their suit. In fact, David pulled (to 4NT) with the South hand, I bid 5♣, he bid 5◇ (to show both red suits), and I passed. Careful play produced eleven tricks for +600.

Assume +600 for five of either minor, and score up 8 IMPs. Five hearts would fail by one trick, so that costs you 8 IMPs. Against 4♠ you would take six tricks for +500 and 6 IMPs (unless South leads a diamond) or +150 (lose 3) if nobody doubled (surely, you didn't pass with the North hand, even with only three hearts?). The datum is rather low because a few North-Souths played 3NT down (on a different auction than the one presented).

Dealer West, Both Vul.
N–S Datum –130

East bids 2◊. If North opened 1NT, 2◊ = ◊ + a major. If South doubles 2◊, West redoubles for rescue, and North and East pass.

```
                    ♠ A K J 9 2
                    ♡ K Q
                    ◊ Q 3 2
                    ♣ J 4 3
      ♠ 8 6 4 3        ┌─────────┐      ♠ —
      ♡ 10 7 6 5       │ N       │      ♡ A 8 4 3
      ◊ 7             │ W     E │      ◊ A J 10 9 8 4
      ♣ Q 7 5 2       │    S    │      ♣ A 10 8
                      └─────────┘
                    ♠ Q 10 7 5
                    ♡ J 9 2
                    ◊ K 6 5
                    ♣ K 9 6
```

DAVID		**LARRY**	
WEST	NORTH	EAST	SOUTH
pass	1NT	2◊	dbl
redbl	pass	pass	2NT
pass	3♠	pass	4♠
pass	pass	dbl	all pass

As you can see, 3NT is easy, but 4♠ is a disaster. Assume you get doubled in four spades and take only eight tricks for –500 and a loss of 9 IMPs. In 3NT you'd probably get a diamond lead and take nine tricks for +600 and a gain of 12 IMPs.

We had lots of excitement on this deal. North opened 1NT and, as East, I overcalled 2◊ (diamonds plus a major). South doubled (cards) and David redoubled (let's hear your major). I decided to leave the redouble in! (Imagine how David felt as he looked at his 4-4-1-4 two-count!) Anyway, South chickened out and ran to 2NT. (It turns out that 2◊ redoubled would have been touch-and-go.) North bid 3♠, South unwisely raised to 4♠, which I doubled for +500 and 12 IMPs (◊A, ruff, two aces and another ruff).

Most of the field played in 4♠ (only half of them were doubled), and there were only two plus scores for North-South. If you doubled 2◊ and stuck out the redouble, you would probably defeat the contract about half the time, so let's call the score for 2◊ redoubled the average of –760 for making and +400 for down one (–180 average for a 2-IMP loss against the datum).

Summary

This final good result propelled us into the money and we went home with the equivalent of about $1,500 between us. Not bad, considering it seemed like we were not in our best form. How was your form with your favorite partner?

Final standings

The top six finishers:

Helgemo–Martens	(Norway, Poland)	+185
Sverrisson–Jorgensen	(Iceland)	+72
Raulund–Pedersen	(Denmark)	+44
Hallberg–Wrang	(Sweden, UK)	+41
Berkowitz–Cohen	(USA)	+37
Koch–Palmund–Auken	(Denmark)	+33

The other ten pairs all finished with negative IMP totals.

Rating guide

- **Minus 20 or more IMPs** — You must have bid this set like David and I did.
- **0 to -20 IMPs** — Not bad; after all, you were bidding against datums achieved by 16 of the best pairs in the world.
- **0 to +20 IMPs** — Well done; your bidding results were better than the average of the participants in Denmark.
- **Plus 20 or more IMPs** — Maybe you should be invited to next year's Politiken Pairs.

Scoring table

North–South datums and vulnerabilities

1. +480	V		**2.** +140	V
3. +320	V		**4.** +170	V
5. +870	V		**6.** +500	V
7. +390	V		**8.** +500	V
9. +340	NV		**10.** +1050	V
11. +280	V		**12.** -180	V
13. +690	NV		**14.** -50	NV
15. +710	NV		**16.** +420	NV
17. +1380	V		**18.** +400	NV
19. +250	V		**20.** -130	V

CAP GEMINI
1999

Have you bid the twenty deals (on pages 164 and 172) that challenged the 1999 participants in the Cap Gemini World Top Tournament? Here are the results and the datum scores from the event, so you can see what your actual score would have been. This time there is a slight twist: Problems 19 and 20 are opening lead problems. So, in this chapter, you can actually score better than your partner on a set of hands that you bid together!

DAVID BERKOWITZ

LARRY COHEN

Deal 1

Dealer East, N–S Vul.
N–S Datum +660

```
              ♠ A 8 3
              ♡ K 7 5
              ◇ Q 6
              ♣ A Q J 9 3
          ┌─────────────┐
          │      N      │
          │ W         E │
          │      S      │
          └─────────────┘
              ♠ K 9 7
              ♡ A J 9 8 2
              ◇ K 7 3 2
              ♣ 7
```

I hope you didn't come out of the gate with your bidding shoes on! Clearly, slam is a bad proposition, and you can assume minus 100 if you reached the six level. Seven of the eight tables in Holland stopped easily enough, but Zia–Forrester bid as follows:

FORRESTER	ZIA
1♡	2♣
2◇	2♡
4♡	4NT
5◇	5♠
5NT	pass

Zia just made eleven tricks. So if you reached the five-level, you have also managed to get out for no swing against the datum of 660. If you reached a slam, however, take a 13-IMP loss; you probably won't make twelve tricks.

Dealer South, N–S Vul.
N–S Datum +940

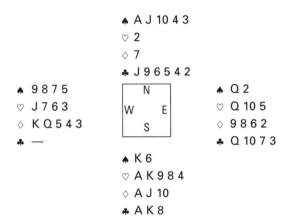

♠ A J 10 4 3
♡ 2
◊ 7
♣ J 9 6 5 4 2

♠ 9 8 7 5
♡ J 7 6 3
◊ K Q 5 4 3
♣ —

♠ Q 2
♡ Q 10 5
◊ 9 8 6 2
♣ Q 10 7 3

♠ K 6
♡ A K 9 8 4
◊ A J 10
♣ A K 8

Most tables started with 2♣ or 2NT and the responder transferred to spades and then showed clubs. Eventually North–South reached 6♣, which was a bit tricky on the actual lie of the cards, but I'll let you be successful. Actually, Helgemo went down from the South side after West showed a two–suiter and led the ◊ K. He drew one trump, ruffed out the ◊ Q, picked up trumps for one loser and discarded two spades from dummy on his ♡ K and ◊ 10. But in the end he played West for the ♠ Q. If you reached any other slam, you'd be down one for minus 100, which costs you 14 IMPs. At a few tables South opened a strong 1♣ and received enemy interference; those tables reached only 5♣ to lose 8 IMPs against the datum of 940. For reaching 6♣, you gain 10 IMPs.

Deal 3

Dealer East, N–S Vul.
N–S Datum +300

East opens 1♡; West bids clubs and East bids 5♣.

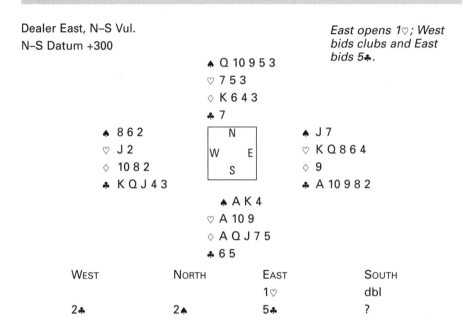

♠ Q 10 9 5 3
♡ 7 5 3
◇ K 6 4 3
♣ 7

♠ 8 6 2
♡ J 2
◇ 10 8 2
♣ K Q J 4 3

♠ J 7
♡ K Q 8 6 4
◇ 9
♣ A 10 9 8 2

♠ A K 4
♡ A 10 9
◇ A Q J 7 5
♣ 6 5

WEST	NORTH	EAST	SOUTH
		1♡	dbl
2♣	2♠	5♣	?

Most auctions started this way, and most Souths doubled and collected only 300. At one table, Holland's Piet Jansen passed 5♣, intending it as forcing, but his partner didn't think so and they collected only 100 (lose 5 IMPs). At one table, Austria's Terri Weigkricht opened the East hand 2♡ to show hearts and a minor. Tony Forrester overcalled 2NT and Doris Fischer bid 3♣ — pass or correct. This was passed around to Forrester who balanced with 3◇, but Zia passed and Tony had to settle for +170. At another table, there was no early enemy bidding and Chagas-Branco started 1NT-2♡ (transfer), 2♠-pass. Then the opponents balanced and Chagas-Branco reached 4♠ for 650.

It's hard for me to suggest a successful auction to the immaculate contract of 6◇. To calculate your score, note that there were twelve easy tricks in diamonds, eleven in spades, and only four on defense against 5♣. The datum was only +300, so if you played in 5♠, you'd actually gain 8 IMPs, despite missing the diamond slam.

Dealer West, Both Vul.
N–S Datum +540

East bids spades and West raises if below 4♠ level.

♠ K Q 8 5
♡ A Q 9 7
◇ 6
♣ Q 9 4 2

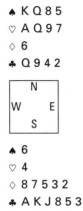

♠ 6
♡ 4
◇ 8 7 5 3 2
♣ A K J 8 5 3

The field auction was a 1♣ opening by North followed by vigorous club support by South. Not everyone drove to 5♣ with the South hand, so the datum was only 540. For reaching 5♣, you gain 2 IMPs. If you reached 3NT, assume down one and deduct 12 IMPs from your score. If you defended against 3♠, you'd collect 200 and lose 8 IMPs. At the two tables that missed the club game, North's club opening didn't promise real clubs, so South didn't bid enough.

Deal 5

Dealer North, Both Vul.
N–S Datum +130

If possible, East opens
1♣, West bids 1♠ and
East 2♠.

```
                    ♠ K 7
                    ♡ K J 7
                    ◊ Q J 7 5
                    ♣ J 6 4 2
    ♠ Q J 9 5 3      ┌─────────┐     ♠ 10 6 4 2
    ♡ 6 5 4 3        │    N    │     ♡ A Q 2
    ◊ 8 4            │ W     E │     ◊ 9 6 3
    ♣ 10 9           │    S    │     ♣ A Q 7
                     └─────────┘
                    ♠ A 8
                    ♡ 10 9 8
                    ◊ A K 10 2
                    ♣ K 8 5 3
```

The trick here was to avoid the awful 3NT contract. If you opened the North hand, the proponents of sound openings will have something nasty to say to you. Of course, even if North passes, those same people won't have much wonderful to say about East's opening that hand either. After North's pass and East's opening, you have a chance to stay out of game, but not much on any other auction.

At our table East passed with his 12-count. I opened 1NT (14–16) in third seat. David drove to 3NT and I received a spade lead. I won in dummy and led a club, hoping for a miracle. East should play low on the club and now I'd need the ♡Q onside for my nine tricks and I'd be down two. However, East made an error by rising with the ♣A to play another spade. I ran the diamonds and went against the odds in the club suit. My best percentage chance was to lead low to the king, hoping East began with A-Q doubleton. But my table feel told me to lead the jack and pin the ten, and we scored a very fortunate 600 to gain 10 IMPs against the datum of +130.

If you played in notrump, assume only seven tricks (sorry). In a minor, assume nine tricks. On defense against spades assume six tricks.

Dealer South, Both Vul.
N–S Datum +280

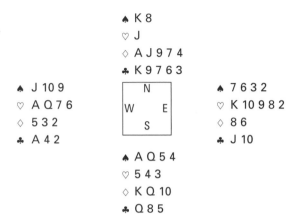

```
                      ♠ K 8
                      ♡ J
                      ◇ A J 9 7 4
                      ♣ K 9 7 6 3
     ♠ J 10 9         ┌─────────┐       ♠ 7 6 3 2
     ♡ A Q 7 6        │    N    │       ♡ K 10 9 8 2
     ◇ 5 3 2          │ W     E │       ◇ 8 6
     ♣ A 4 2          │    S    │       ♣ J 10
                      └─────────┘
                      ♠ A Q 5 4
                      ♡ 5 4 3
                      ◇ K Q 10
                      ♣ Q 8 5
```

The Polish world champions, Kwiecien-Pszczola, overreached to 6◇ down one (lose 9 IMPs), and Chagas-Branco played in 3NT off the first six tricks (lose 10 IMPs). Westra-Leufkens reached the sexy 4-2 spade fit, and made 620. True, 4♠ can be defeated, but at the table there were lots of chances to make it, and if you somehow reached that spot, take 620 and 8 IMPs for being so imaginative.

The rest of the field played in 5♣ or 5◇. A few declarers received a spade lead and made the contract easily by getting rid of the heart loser. At the tables where hearts were led, declarer had to guess clubs. All declarers led a club from the North hand. Second hand played the ten and the queen lost to the ace. Four out of five declarers subsequently guessed correctly that the J-10 was doubleton. It would have been much tougher if the West player ducked the ♣Q smoothly. Then declarer would probably misguess on the next round. In any event, since almost everyone was successful, assume eleven tricks if you played in either minor (winning 8 IMPs if you were in game), ten tricks in spades, and seven tricks in notrump. The datum was +280.

Deal 7

Dealer West, Neither Vul.
N–S Datum +290

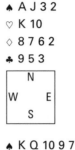

```
              ♠ A J 3 2
              ♡ K 10
              ◇ 8 7 6 2
              ♣ 9 5 3

              ♠ K Q 10 9 7
              ♡ A 9 7 6
              ◇ A
              ♣ 7 6 4
```

LARRY		**DAVID**	
WEST	NORTH	EAST	SOUTH
pass	pass	pass	1♠
pass	2♠	all pass	

Chagas–Branco stopped in 2♠ against us. Personally, I think the North hand with its four trumps is worth using Drury to show a passed-hand limit raise. About half the field reached the laydown game, some of them after an opening bid in front of the South hand. The datum was +290, so you either lost 3 IMPs or won 4 IMPs depending on whether you reached the spade game. If you played in notrump, however, there were only eight tricks.

Dealer West, N–S Vul.
N–S Datum +240

West opens 3♠; East bids 4♠ if possible.

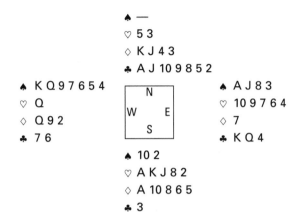

```
                    ♠ —
                    ♡ 5 3
                    ◇ K J 4 3
                    ♣ A J 10 9 8 5 2
  ♠ K Q 9 7 6 5 4         ┌─────────┐    ♠ A J 8 3
  ♡ Q                     │    N    │    ♡ 10 9 7 6 4
  ◇ Q 9 2                 │ W     E │    ◇ 7
  ♣ 7 6                   │    S    │    ♣ K Q 4
                          └─────────┘
                    ♠ 10 2
                    ♡ A K J 8 2
                    ◇ A 10 8 6 5
                    ♣ 3
```

There were lots of different auctions on this one! At one table it went:

WEST	NORTH	EAST	SOUTH
3♠	pass	4♠	all pass

This was down one, a poor result for North-South, who can make 6◇.

WEST	NORTH	EAST	SOUTH
3♠	4♣	4♠	?

What about this auction with the South hand? At two tables South bid 4NT for takeout and 6◇ was reached. Others doubled 4♠ and now it was up to North to do the right thing, but most Norths passed or retreated to 5♣.

WEST	NORTH	EAST	SOUTH
3♠	pass	4♠	dbl

South's double caused North to bid 6♣, down one, for an 8-IMP loss against the datum of +240. If you reached 6◇, you gain a whopping 15 IMPs. I'll assume you make 6◇, as your reward for reaching it. You ruff the spade lead and play a heart to the ace, dropping the queen. Now club to the ace, club ruff, spade ruff and club ruff low — if West overruffs, you're OK. But he pitches! Still, you know he's 7-1-3-2, so you lead to the ◇J and play a high club.

Deal 9

Dealer West, E–W Vul.
N–S Datum +370

        ♠ A 8
        ♡ Q 6 4 3
        ◇ Q 6 3 2
        ♣ A 7 3

```
        N
    W       E
        S
```

        ♠ Q 3
        ♡ A K J 7 5 2
        ◇ A 10 9 7
        ♣ 9

Six out of the eight pairs stopped successfully in a heart game, so the datum was a healthy +370. The cards were rather unfriendly, including a 4-1 diamond break. Assume only ten tricks in diamonds (one pair played 5◇ down one for a loss of 10 IMPs). In hearts, eleven tricks were available, so bidding game in hearts gained you 2 IMPs.

Dealer North, E–W Vul.
N–S Datum –70

<pre>
                    ♠ A 2
                    ♡ A K J 8 7 3 2
                    ◊ A 10 7
                    ♣ J
                  ┌─────────┐
                  │   N   │
                  │ W   E │
                  │   S   │
                  └─────────┘
                    ♠ Q 4
                    ♡ Q 6
                    ◊ J 6 5 4 3 2
                    ♣ A K 4
</pre>

We played this deal in 6◊ by South after David opened the North hand with a big club. I received a heart lead and won with the queen to play a diamond toward dummy's A-10-7. West played low, and I couldn't afford to finesse the ten for fear of a heart ruff. I played the ◊A and another diamond, but alas, the K-Q-9 were offside — so there was no way to make the slam.

Slam (in either red suit) is certainly above 50%, so normally I wouldn't include such a deal in this book. Usually I use deals where you get rewarded for bidding to the proper contract. Here, I expected to lose IMPs, since surely some of the field would miss the slam. Boy, was I ever wrong. In fact, half the field, yes, four pairs, reached seven hearts, typically after South showed diamonds and North Blackwooded. The datum was –70 so you gain an IMP for stopping in six, and you gain 10 or 11 lucky IMPs for stopping in 5◊ or 5♡ respectively.

Deal 11

Dealer South, E–W Vul.
N–S Datum +30

<pre>
                    ♠ A 8 7 4
                    ♡ A Q 3
                    ◇ 9 4
                    ♣ A J 8 6
                 ┌─────────────┐
                 │   N   │
                 │ W   E │
                 │   S   │
                 └─────────────┘
                    ♠ K 6 5 3
                    ♡ K J 9
                    ◇ A Q J 10 8
                    ♣ 5
</pre>

Clearly this slam is less than 50%. It needs 3-2 spades and the diamond finesse. Spades were 3-2, but the ◇K was wrong so stopping in game (or in 5♠) was worth 9 IMPs. The datum score was only +30, because six of the eight pairs over-reached to 6♠. Most auctions started 1◇-1♠, 3♠, after which many Norths drove to slam. Holland's Anton Maas chose to bid only 4♠ after the usual start and he was rewarded with +450 and 9 IMPs. Gabriel Chagas was the other North player to take the low road; he chose to cuebid over 3♠, but didn't drive to slam.

Dealer North, Neither Vul.
N–S Datum +430

$\spadesuit$ K Q 9 5 4 2
$\heartsuit$ —
$\diamond$ J 10 8
$\clubsuit$ A Q 9 2

```
        N
    W       E
        S
```

$\spadesuit$ A 6
$\heartsuit$ K Q 9 6 3
$\diamond$ A K 6
$\clubsuit$ 10 8 7

On the lie of the cards, ten tricks are the limit in either spades or notrump. The field handled this deal well; four pairs stopped in 3NT and the other four played in 4$\spadesuit$. Any wrong step and you lose 10 IMPs against the datum of +430.

Deal 13

Dealer East, N–S Vul.
N–S Datum +800

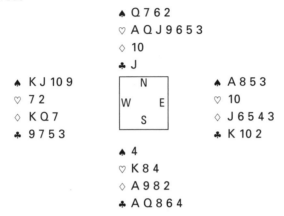

```
                    ♠ Q 7 6 2
                    ♡ A Q J 9 6 5 3
                    ◇ 10
                    ♣ J
    ♠ K J 10 9          N          ♠ A 8 5 3
    ♡ 7 2        W          E       ♡ 10
    ◇ K Q 7             S          ◇ J 6 5 4 3
    ♣ 9 7 5 3                       ♣ K 10 2
                    ♠ 4
                    ♡ K 8 4
                    ◇ A 9 8 2
                    ♣ A Q 8 6 4
```

Six hearts is odds-on, and on the lie of the cards there was no way to prevent 1430. Only two pairs reached the good slam. I gave our side no chance when I responded 4♡ to David's Precision 1◇ opening. Facing a limited opener (with possibly a doubleton diamond), I decided that slam was unlikely and wasn't worth investigating, given that a 1♡ response would make it easy for the favorable-vulnerability opponents to find a good sacrifice in five of a minor. If I had responded 1♡, we might have had a chance.

Obviously, others found the 23-point slam tough to reach too, so we fortunately lost only 3 IMPs against the datum.

Dealer South, N–S Vul.
N–S Datum +1950

♠ J 9 4 2
♡ K J
◇ A 3
♣ A K 10 9 6

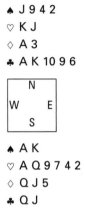

♠ A K
♡ A Q 9 7 4 2
◇ Q J 5
♣ Q J

We had a long, torturous Precision auction on VuGraph to 7♣. I held the ♣Q-J and learned that David had ♣A-K-x-x-x, ♡K-x and the ◇A. Not knowing about the ♡J, I elected for the safe IMP contract of 7♣ rather than trying for a super-maximum score in 7NT. Similarly, Norway's Tor Helness held the North hand and elected to play in hearts, when he learned that his partner held ace-queen fifth. Yes, I see that South has six hearts, but Geir Helgemo opened the South hand 2NT and then showed a five-card heart suit over Puppet Stayman (there's no way to show six!). Anyway, all the key jacks were there, so 7♣, 7♡ and 7NT were all cold.

Two of the Dutch pairs had a quantitative auction and stopped in 6NT, and the Italian world champions, Buratti-Lanzarotti, stopped in 4♡! The datum was 'only' +1950, so bidding the grand slam was worth a decent pickup. Scoring: 7NT, win 7 IMPs; 7♡, win 6 IMPs; 7♣, win 5 IMPs; 6NT or 6♡, lose 10 IMPs; 6♣, lose 11 IMPs.

Deal 15

Dealer East, N–S Vul.
N–S Datum +1830

West bids 2♠.

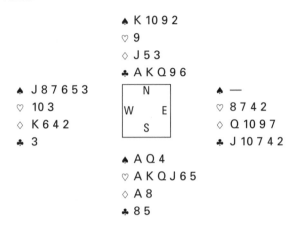

♠ K 10 9 2
♡ 9
◇ J 5 3
♣ A K Q 9 6

♠ J 8 7 6 5 3
♡ 10 3
◇ K 6 4 2
♣ 3

♠ —
♡ 8 7 4 2
◇ Q 10 9 7
♣ J 10 7 4 2

♠ A Q 4
♡ A K Q J 6 5
◇ A 8
♣ 8 5

ZIA	VERSACE	FORRESTER	LAURIA
West	North	East	South
		pass	2♣
2♠	2NT	pass	3♡
pass	4NT	all pass	

This time it was Lauria–Versace who had trouble. Obviously 4NT was intended as Blackwood and taken as natural. The Polish world champions, Kwiecien-Pszczola, bid to 7♡ by South, which was due to fail by a trick (the opening spade lead gets ruffed). However, a Lightner double chased them into 7NT for 2220 and a 9–IMP pickup. If you reached a heart contract by South, sorry, only twelve tricks — lose 9 IMPs for 6♡ and 18 big ones for the grand slam. (After the 2♠ overcall it's not too surprising to get a 6-0 break.)

There are thirteen easy tricks in notrump, so 7NT is worth a 9–IMP gain against the datum of 1830, while 6 NT costs you 5 IMPs.

Dealer North, Both Vul.
N–S Datum +730

East bids diamonds, West bids minimum number of spades (not forcing).

```
                        ♠ A 6 5 2
                        ♡ 6 4
                        ◇ A 9 5 2
                        ♣ J 10 9
   ♠ K Q 10 9 8 7 3   ┌─────────┐   ♠ J
   ♡ 5 2              │    N    │   ♡ A J 9 7 3
   ◇ J 6             │ W     E │   ◇ K Q 10 8 4 3
   ♣ 4 2              │    S    │   ♣ K
                      └─────────┘
                        ♠ 4
                        ♡ K Q 10 8
                        ◇ 7
                        ♣ A Q 8 7 6 5 3
```

Based on East's opening bid, 6♣ is an odds–on favorite, and in fact twelve tricks were easy. However, reaching a slam after an opponent's opening bid and response is not so simple. None of the eight pairs in the Hague scored 1370. Four pairs played a more boring 5♣ and claimed 620 early in the play (lose 3 IMPs). Four pairs collected numbers, three of which were 500, 800, and 1100, against 5♠ doubled, 4◇ doubled, and 5◇ doubled, respectively (scoring minus 8 IMPs, plus 2 IMPs, and plus 9 IMPs respectively). But the big news was the fourth number: 2300! Against 4♡ doubled, by East, the defense took eleven tricks to score a whopping 17 IMPs against the datum of +730.

How is this possible? South led the ♣A and a low club, on which declarer pitched her stiff spade. A trump came through to the nine and ten. South played a spade to the ace, ruffed. Declarer led a diamond to the jack and ace. North returned his second trump. Declarer won the ace and could have played on diamonds for down 800, but played a trump, which would lead to –500 or –2300.

The E-W datum was –730 so the IMP odds were about like this:

–500	=	Win 6
–800	=	Lose 2
–2300	=	Lose 17

Declarer probably thought hearts were 3–3, since it looked as if North was 4-3-3-3 or 4-3-2-4. Anyway, the play risked 15 IMPs in an effort to save 8 — not quite as bad as it looks!

Deal 17

Dealer East, E–W Vul.
N–S Datum –30

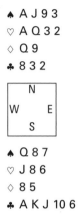

♠ A J 9 3
♡ A Q 3 2
◇ Q 9
♣ 8 3 2

♠ Q 8 7
♡ J 8 6
◇ 8 5
♣ A K J 10 6

I keep referring to those proponents of sound openings, and this one should keep them happy. At two tables South opened a very light 1♣ and North drove to the doomed 3NT. At another table, I opened a 10-12 notrump and, when David invited, I continued to 3NT anyway (I had a nice 11, I thought).

After passing the South hand it's much easier to stop low, but you'd better stop in 1NT or 3♣, since the limit of the hand is seven tricks in notrump and nine in clubs. You'd also make eight tricks in spades or hearts if you ended up in your 4-3 fit. The datum was –30, so stopping in a successful partscore is worth about 4 IMPs.

Dealer East, Both Vul.
N–S Datum +460

West bids 1♡ if possible.

```
                    ♠ A 10 8 6
                    ♡ Q 5 2
                    ◇ 8 4 3
                    ♣ 10 8 2
   ♠ K 4 2            ┌─────────┐        ♠ Q J 5
   ♡ K J 10 9 3       │    N    │        ♡ 8 7 6
   ◇ Q 10 9 5         │ W     E │        ◇ J 6 2
   ♣ 9               │    S    │        ♣ K 5 4 3
                    └─────────┘
                    ♠ 9 7 3
                    ♡ A 4
                    ◇ A K 7
                    ♣ A Q J 7 6
```

The ♡K and ♣K were favorably located, so ten tricks were easy in 3NT after a heart lead. Clearly this vulnerable game is worth bidding.

After 1♣ –1♡ (overcall) it's not clear that North should make a negative double. If he does, I believe that South should drive to game with his excellent controls and source of tricks. Even if North passes, South can reopen with 1NT, get a raise to 2NT by North and then, well, where there are eight tricks, there are usually nine.

The datum was +460, so missing this game is costly and you lose 7 IMPs if you stopped in a notrump partscore. Reaching game nets you a 5-IMP gain.

Deal 19

Dealer East, Neither Vul.
N–S Datum +660

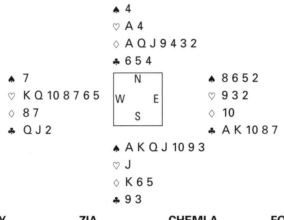

	♠ 4	
	♡ A 4	
	◊ A Q J 9 4 3 2	
	♣ 6 5 4	

♠ 7		♠ 8 6 5 2
♡ K Q 10 8 7 6 5		♡ 9 3 2
◊ 8 7		◊ 10
♣ Q J 2		♣ A K 10 8 7

	♠ A K Q J 10 9 3	
	♡ J	
	◊ K 6 5	
	♣ 9 3	

LEVY	ZIA	CHEMLA	FORRESTER
WEST	NORTH	EAST	SOUTH
		pass	1♠
3♡	3NT	4♡	4NT
pass	6◊	pass	6NT
pass	pass	dbl	7♠
all pass			

This hand was the talk of the tournament. I think a club lead is a standout, but France's Alain Levy led the king of hearts and his irritable partner, Paul Chemla, can still be heard cursing in French. Zia spread his hand and claimed 1510.

At another table, West also led the ♡K against 6NT doubled to go minus 1330 (not a number you see every day). The best bid by East was made by Massimo Lanzarotti. Check out his 4♣ call:

BURATTI	HELGEMO	LANZAROTTI	HELNESS
WEST	NORTH	EAST	SOUTH
		pass	1♠
3♡	3NT	4♣!	4♠
5♡	dbl	all pass	

Playing 5♡ doubled was worth −100 and a gain of 11 IMPs for the Italians. At our table we played a calm spade game and lost 4 IMPs for +510, against the +660 datum. If you found a club lead (without partner's help!), take 13 IMPs. If you led anything else, lose 13 IMPs and incur the wrath of *L'Enfant Terrible*.

Dealer South, N–S Vul.
N–S Datum +670

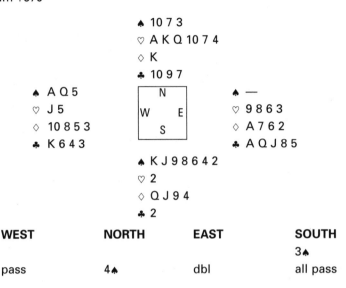

```
                        ♠ 10 7 3
                        ♡ A K Q 10 7 4
                        ◇ K
                        ♣ 10 9 7
    ♠ A Q 5         ┌─────────┐      ♠ —
    ♡ J 5           │    N    │      ♡ 9 8 6 3
    ◇ 10 8 5 3      │ W     E │      ◇ A 7 6 2
    ♣ K 6 4 3       │    S    │      ♣ A Q J 8 5
                    └─────────┘
                        ♠ K J 9 8 6 4 2
                        ♡ 2
                        ◇ Q J 9 4
                        ♣ 2
```

WEST	NORTH	EAST	SOUTH
			3♠
pass	4♠	dbl	all pass

This hand amazed me. I think this is a solvable lead problem, especially for the world's best players. The dummy has raised to 4♠ without much in spades or highcards. Probably dummy will have a long, strong red suit on which declarer can take discards. The lead of the ♠A (to examine dummy) or a club (unlikely to be dummy's suit) seem like standouts, and would lead to +200. Six out of the seven players who had this lead problem chose the ♡J and were minus 790 (lose 3 IMPs). Only Geir Helgemo found the club lead to win 13 IMPs.

Summary

Final standings

Berkowitz–Cohen	(USA)	+136
Buratti–Lanzarotti	(Italy)	+83
Leufkens–Westra	(Holland)	+80
Helgemo–Helness	(Norway)	+72
Chagas–Branco	(Brazil)	+52
Lauria–Versace	(Italy)	+43
Mahmood–Forrester	(USA–UK)	+21
Kwiecien–Pszczola	(Poland)	+8

Yes, we finally won after years of trying!

Rating guide

- **Minus 20 IMPs or more**   Brush up your partnership.
- **0 to -20 IMPs**   Well, it was a tough set.
- **0 to +20 IMPs**   Nicely done.
- **Plus 20 to 40 IMPs**   You're the tough ones.
- **Plus 40 IMPS or more**   You should be playing at the Hague!

Scoring table

North–South datums and vulnerabilities

1. +660	V		**2.** +940	V	
3. +300	V		**4.** +540	V	
5. +130	V		**6.** +280	V	
7. +290	NV		**8.** +240	V	
9. +370	NV		**10** -70	NV	
11. +30	NV		**12.** +430	NV	
13. +800	V		**14.** +1950	V	
15. +1830	V		**16.** +730	V	
17. -30	NV		**18.** +460	V	

19. Club lead: win 13 IMPs, others lose 13.
20. Black-suit lead: win 13 IMPs, others lose 3.

CAP GEMINI 2000

The 2000 edition of the Cap Gemini World Top 16 Tournament, unlike the previous year's event, was full of drama. This time the championship went down to the final deal. Zia Mahmood and Andy Robson narrowly edged out Bobby Levin and Steve Weinstein (see Robson's Introduction to this book, where he presents the critical last deal). To illustrate what a tough event this is, it's sad for me to say that the top three pairs in 1999 all finished at the bottom of the pack in 2000. At the end of this chapter the top finishers are listed, and you won't see my name among them. Only the top six finishers get automatically invited back for next year, so this looks like a good place to end this book. If you are bidding along with us, you are East-West this time and the hands are on pages 165 and 173.

ANDREW ROBSON

ZIA MAHMOOD

Deal 1

Dealer North, N–S Vul.
E–W Datum –20

North opens 1♠. If possible, South bids 1NT, North 2◊ and South 3◊.

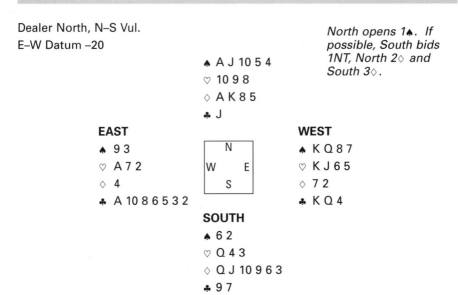

```
                    ♠ A J 10 5 4
                    ♡ 10 9 8
                    ◊ A K 8 5
                    ♣ J

   EAST                                    WEST
   ♠ 9 3              ┌─────────┐          ♠ K Q 8 7
   ♡ A 7 2            │    N    │          ♡ K J 6 5
   ◊ 4               W│        E│          ◊ 7 2
   ♣ A 10 8 6 5 3 2   │    S    │          ♣ K Q 4
                      └─────────┘
                    SOUTH
                    ♠ 6 2
                    ♡ Q 4 3
                    ◊ Q J 10 9 6 3
                    ♣ 9 7
```

This is a tough one. I wouldn't overcall 1NT over 1♠ with the East hand, so I would pass. Now if South responds a forcing notrump, West might overcall 2♣, and East can cuebid 2♠ over North's 2◊ rebid. After that start, both East and West would have to take optimistic views to reach 5♣. From East's point of view he is off all four aces and maybe the first two diamond tricks. From West's point of view, it's difficult to picture eleven tricks when East couldn't act over the 1♠ opening.

None of the eight pairs reached 5♣. Four North-South pairs bought it in a diamond partial (nine tricks) and three East-Wests played a club partial (11 tricks). The remaining East-West pair played in 3NT, and lost the first seven tricks. The E–W datum was –20, so bidding 5♣ is worth 9 IMPs. Even buying the hand in a club partial is worth 5 IMPs.

Dealer East, E–W Vul.
E–W Datum +300.

South opens 1♣.

```
                  ♠ 7 5 3
                  ♡ 10 8 4
                  ◇ K 10 3 2
                  ♣ 9 4 2
    EAST                              WEST
    ♠ A Q J       ┌──────────┐       ♠ K 10 8 2
    ♡ K Q 9 7 5 2 │    N     │       ♡ J 3
    ◇ A 9 6       │ W      E │       ◇ Q J 8 7
    ♣ 10          │    S     │       ♣ J 7 3
                  └──────────┘
                  SOUTH
                  ♠ 9 6 4
                  ♡ A 6
                  ◇ 5 4
                  ♣ A K Q 8 6 5
```

Half the field stopped in a partial, so bidding 4♡ is an 8-IMP gain against the datum of +300. After South's 1♣ West can either overcall 1♡, or make a takeout double. Basically, at the tables where West started with a simple overcall, game was missed. When West started with a double, game was reached.

Two Souths opened with a creative 1NT; this resulted in both opposing Wests making a simple overcall and missing a game. One East–West pair failed in 4♡ when North led a club and South won and shifted to a diamond. Declarer grabbed his ace and went down one when the defense got a diamond ruff. Ducking the diamond would have led to plus 620. If you reached either major, you can assume ten tricks and win 8 IMPs if you bid game (lose 4 if you didn't).

Deal 3

Dealer East, N–S Vul.
E–W Datum +220

South bids 1♠.

```
              ♠ 2
              ♡ Q 9 6
              ◇ 10 6 3
              ♣ 9 8 7 5 3 2
  ♠ J 4          ┌─────────┐      ♠ A K Q 3
  ♡ K 7 4        │    N    │      ♡ J 8 5 3 2
  ◇ A 8 4 2      │ W     E │      ◇ Q 9 5
  ♣ Q J 10 4     │    S    │      ♣ K
                 └─────────┘
              ♠ 10 9 8 7 6 5
              ♡ A 10
              ◇ K J 7
              ♣ A 6
```

Three notrump makes easily and you can assume +400 and pick up 5 IMPs if you reached that contract. Four hearts is inferior and you can presume –50 (lose 7). The declarers in 4♡ were defeated by a spade lead and two spade ruffs (the second one promoted the trump queen).

After the start of 1♡ by East and a 1♠ overcall, there are two ways to reach notrump. One is for West to bid 2♠ (heart raise) and for East to bid notrump. The other is for West to start with a negative double and for East to bid notrump. The problem, of course, is that East is too strong to make a minimum rebid in notrump, but too weak to jump in notrump. One East compromised by passing the negative double of 1♠ and he collected +200 and lost 1 IMP against the datum of +220.

It's actually interesting that good defense should defeat 1♠ two tricks for 500. Suppose West leads the ♣Q. If declarer leads a trump, West wins and continues clubs, noting partner's discouraging heart signal. East can win the next trump lead, cash trumps, and lead a heart. Even if declarer plays the ♡A and a heart, West can win and lead a low diamond. East, knowing that South started with three diamonds, should put in the ◇9. Thus declarer loses four spades, one heart, two diamonds and one club.

Dealer East, Both Vul.
E–W Datum +650

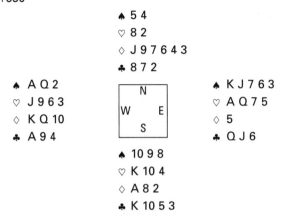

```
                    ♠ 5 4
                    ♡ 8 2
                    ◇ J 9 7 6 4 3
                    ♣ 8 7 2
   ♠ A Q 2                          ♠ K J 7 6 3
   ♡ J 9 6 3          N             ♡ A Q 7 5
   ◇ K Q 10      W         E        ◇ 5
   ♣ A 9 4           S             ♣ Q J 6
                    ♠ 10 9 8
                    ♡ K 10 4
                    ◇ A 8 2
                    ♣ K 10 5 3
```

Only one pair overreached to a slam, so the datum was 650 (the high and low scores are thrown out and the middle six are averaged to produce the datum). If East–West uncover the heart fit, it is easy to avoid the slam by using Roman Key Card Blackwood — two key cards are missing, which is good enough reason to stay out. Bidding slam will cost aggressive pairs 13 IMPs; staying in game just means you don't lose any!

Deal 5

Dealer North, Both Vul.
E–W Datum +1040

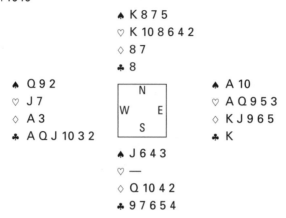

```
                          ♠ K 8 7 5
                          ♡ K 10 8 6 4 2
                          ◊ 8 7
                          ♣ 8
        ♠ Q 9 2              ┌─────────┐        ♠ A 10
        ♡ J 7               │    N    │        ♡ A Q 9 5 3
        ◊ A 3               │ W     E │        ◊ K J 9 6 5
        ♣ A Q J 10 3 2      │    S    │        ♣ K
                            └─────────┘
                          ♠ J 6 4 3
                          ♡ —
                          ◊ Q 10 4 2
                          ♣ 9 7 6 5 4
```

There were five pairs scoring 1440 in 6NT. Six clubs is slightly better (a few extra chances) but it might fail on a heart lead, ruffed. Take 1370 if you reached 6♣ (win 8 IMPs) and 1440 for 6NT (win 10 IMPs). A few Norths opened 2♡ and a few more opened Multi to show a weak two in either major. After that start some of the East-Wests ended up in hearts against the 6-0 break! One East-West pair reached the startling contract of 6♡ but North, who obviously couldn't stand prosperity, foolishly doubled and chased them to the making 6NT.

Without any interference the auction begins

WEST	EAST
	1♡
2♣	2◊
?	

Now, West can bid 3♣ if it is forcing and East can then invite with a quantitative 4NT. With his good suit West can accept the invitation and bid the slam. The datum was 1040, so many IMPs swing on your slam–bidding decision on this deal.

Dealer East, Neither Vul.
E–W Datum +690

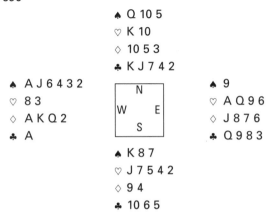

```
              ♠ Q 10 5
              ♡ K 10
              ◊ 10 5 3
              ♣ K J 7 4 2
♠ A J 6 4 3 2    ┌─────────┐    ♠ 9
♡ 8 3            │    N    │    ♡ A Q 9 6
◊ A K Q 2        │ W     E │    ◊ J 8 7 6
♣ A              │    S    │    ♣ Q 9 8 3
                 └─────────┘
              ♠ K 8 7
              ♡ J 7 5 4 2
              ◊ 9 4
              ♣ 10 6 5
```

This deal hinged on West's rebid after 1♠–1NT. I think the hand warrants a jump shift to 3◊. This is a very offensive (and I mean that in a positive bridge sense) 18-count and any lesser rebid does not do the hand justice. Over West's 3◊ I think East should raise to 4◊ and from that start 6◊ should be reached. Note that if West bids 4♠ over 4◊, though, East should pass (West may be 6-3-3-1, for example), so in order to move forward West must either take a chance on the heart control or cuebid 5♣.

Because of the favorable lie of the cards, 7◊ is a make, so if you stumbled into that contract you get a lucky pickup of 16 IMPs. Just reaching 6◊ is worth 6 IMPs because only half the field played in slam. Spades will make eleven tricks, so lose 1 IMP for playing in 4♠, and 2 IMPs for 5◊. You'll even make 3NT if you stumble into it, so lose only 3 IMPs if you did.

Deal 7

Dealer East, E–W Vul.
E–W Datum +130

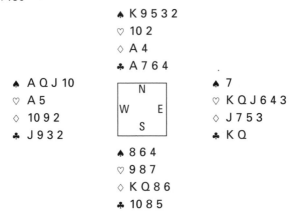

```
                        ♠ K 9 5 3 2
                        ♡ 10 2
                        ◇ A 4
                        ♣ A 7 6 4
  ♠ A Q J 10                              ♠ 7
  ♡ A 5            ┌─────────┐            ♡ K Q J 6 4 3
  ◇ 10 9 2        │    N    │            ◇ J 7 5 3
  ♣ J 9 3 2      │ W     E │            ♣ K Q
                  │    S    │
                  └─────────┘
                        ♠ 8 6 4
                        ♡ 9 8 7
                        ◇ K Q 8 6
                        ♣ 10 8 5
```

Good bidding was its own reward on this deal. The five pairs that reached 4♡ (1♡-1♠, 2♡-4♡) were down one. The three pairs that reached 3NT all scored +600. With North on lead, only the double-dummy ◇A lead (followed by two more diamonds and then a spade) defeats 3NT. But with South on lead, a low diamond to the ace and a diamond back allows South to cash a third diamond and switch to a spade. So take down one (lose 6 IMPs) if you bid it from the East position, but count on nine tricks if West was declarer, and win 10 IMPs.

West	East
	1♡
1♠	2♡
?	

In this sequence, some pairs play that 2NT is forcing. That would be one possible start to reach 3NT, and another is for West to rebid 3♣ over 2♡ and now East might bid 3NT or, better, 3◇.

Dealer North, E–W Vul.
E–W Datum +20

North opens 3♡.

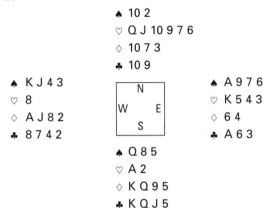

♠ 10 2
♡ Q J 10 9 7 6
◇ 10 7 3
♣ 10 9

♠ K J 4 3
♡ 8
◇ A J 8 2
♣ 8 7 4 2

♠ A 9 7 6
♡ K 5 4 3
◇ 6 4
♣ A 6 3

♠ Q 8 5
♡ A 2
◇ K Q 9 5
♣ K Q J 5

These days, at favorable vulnerability many North players open 3♡ (it's too weak for 2♡)! In fact three of the eight Norths chose this action. At two tables the deal played there (presume seven tricks and win 1 IMP). At the third table West balanced with a takeout double and East jumped to 4♠, which got doubled and went down 500.

If West doubles 3♡, I think East should pass. Opposite a presumed 4-1-4-4 shape there are only 16 Total Trumps (8 spades East–West and 8 hearts North–South). The Law of Total Tricks says that makes bidding 4♠ a big loser in the long run. If 4♠ is making, the penalty against 3♡ should be quite sufficient. In this case neither side could make too many tricks, so defending was a big winner.

At half the tables North opened with a two-level preempt and South usually tried for game and stopped in 3♡ down two. The datum is +20, so collecting 100 is worth 2 IMPs; collecting 300 is worth 7 IMPs, but going minus 500 in 3NT doubled or 4♠ doubled costs 11 IMPs.

Deal 9

Dealer East, Both Vul.
E–W Datum –20

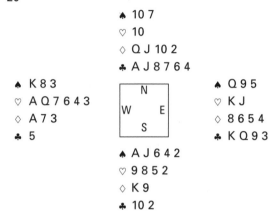

```
                        ♠ 10 7
                        ♡ 10
                        ♢ Q J 10 2
                        ♣ A J 8 7 6 4
        ♠ K 8 3                          ♠ Q 9 5
        ♡ A Q 7 6 4 3        N           ♡ K J
        ♢ A 7 3          W       E       ♢ 8 6 5 4
        ♣ 5                  S           ♣ K Q 9 3
                        ♠ A J 6 4 2
                        ♡ 9 8 5 2
                        ♢ K 9
                        ♣ 10 2
```

The field reached game, but 4♡ fails (presume -100) so the datum is –20. The auction usually starts

WEST	EAST
	pass
1♡	1NT
2♡	?

Because West is in third seat, his sequence of 1♡ followed by 2♡ should show a good hand (in third seat you can open 2♡ with a fairly decent hand). If East jumps to 4♡, diamonds are led and the game must fail. Presume nine tricks in either notrump or hearts. Reaching 3NT gives you a gain of 11 IMPs.

Dealer South, N–S Vul.
E–W Datum +430

South opens 2♡ and North bids 3♡.

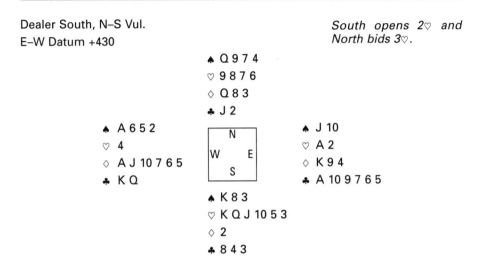

```
                    ♠ Q 9 7 4
                    ♡ 9 8 7 6
                    ◇ Q 8 3
                    ♣ J 2
      ♠ A 6 5 2                      ♠ J 10
      ♡ 4              N             ♡ A 2
      ◇ A J 10 7 6 5  W   E         ◇ K 9 4
      ♣ K Q             S            ♣ A 10 9 7 6 5
                    ♠ K 8 3
                    ♡ K Q J 10 5 3
                    ◇ 2
                    ♣ 8 4 3
```

This is an excellent (but hard to reach) slam in either minor. On a spade lead you have to guess the ◇Q, but I'll let you presume that you would be successful (playing the preemptor for a singleton).

Only one pair reached the slam. Lorenzo Lauria doubled 2♡ and Alfredo Versace made a responsive double of the raise to 3♡. West was now able to bid 4◇, forcing (see Deal 13), and the slam was reached. The most common auction was for West to overcall 3◇ and East simply to bid 3NT. At matchpoints that might make sense, but at IMPs, East can expect that at least 5◇ will make, so I think he should move towards five or six diamonds.

Score yourself as follows: 6♣ or 6◇, 10 IMPs; 5♣ or 5◇, 0 IMPs; 3NT, 0 IMPs.

Deal 11

Dealer West, Both Vul.
E–W Datum +140

North bids 2◇.

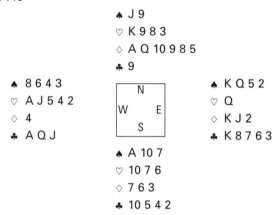

```
                    ♠ J 9
                    ♡ K 9 8 3
                    ◇ A Q 10 9 8 5
                    ♣ 9
    ♠ 8 6 4 3          ┌─────────┐          ♠ K Q 5 2
    ♡ A J 5 4 2        │    N    │          ♡ Q
    ◇ 4              W │         │ E        ◇ K J 2
    ♣ A Q J            │    S    │          ♣ K 8 7 6 3
                       └─────────┘
                    ♠ A 10 7
                    ♡ 10 7 6
                    ◇ 7 6 3
                    ♣ 10 5 4 2
```

This deal isn't really fair, but that's life. If you reached 4♠ (as six of the eight pairs did) you are down one and lose 6 IMPs. If you reached 3NT (as two of the eight pairs did), you are +600 to gain 10 IMPs against the datum of +140. If the over-caller has both high diamonds, 3NT is almost sure to make (the analysis is complicated, but declarer will normally emerge with nine tricks). Five declarers in 4♠ were defeated by a club ruff. The defenders took their diamond ace, South's two natural trump tricks, and North's ruff.

Poland's Krzysztof Jassem made the play of the tournament with the West cards in 4♠. He won the singleton club lead in hand. A spade to the king would have led to a swift down one, but he played a diamond at Trick 2. North won and wanted to reach his partner for a club ruff. He shifted to a spade. Which spade? If North shifts to the spade nine and dummy plays low, South would be hard-pressed to put in the ten! North actually played the ♠J. Jassem countered with the brilliant play of ducking in dummy! This prevented South from winning his trump ace at the right time to give his partner a ruff. Thus declarer avoided a defensive club ruff and was the only one to make his spade game.

Dealer North, E–W Vul.
E–W Datum +2210

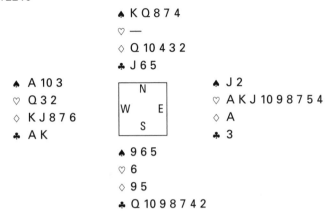

```
                        ♠ K Q 8 7 4
                        ♡ —
                        ◊ Q 10 4 3 2
                        ♣ J 6 5
   ♠ A 10 3          ┌─────────┐        ♠ J 2
   ♡ Q 3 2           │   N     │        ♡ A K J 10 9 8 7 5 4
   ◊ K J 8 7 6       │ W     E │        ◊ A
   ♣ A K             │   S     │        ♣ 3
                     └─────────┘
                        ♠ 9 6 5
                        ♡ 6
                        ◊ 9 5
                        ♣ Q 10 9 8 7 4 2
```

With a free run this hand is easy. Whether East opens 1♡, 4♣ (Namyats) or 2♣, it's easy to Blackwood into the laydown grand (in hearts or notrump). At a few tables North opened with a two-level spade preempt. Two Easts jumped to 4♡ and West Blackwooded. I think East might be too strong for 4♡ and a couple of players agreed by doubling the 2♠ bid. However, all eight tables reached the grand (only one pair played notrump) and the datum was 2210.

Deal 13

Dealer North, E–W Vul.
E–W Datum +620

North opens 2♠.

```
              ♠ A Q 9 7 6 5 3
              ♡ J 6
              ◊ 8 7
              ♣ J 3
  ♠ J 10            N           ♠ 8 2
  ♡ Q 10 9 8 5    W   E         ♡ A
  ◊ A Q 9 5 4         S         ◊ 3 2
  ♣ 6                           ♣ A K Q 8 7 5 4 2
              ♠ K 4
              ♡ K 7 4 3 2
              ◊ K J 10 6
              ♣ 10 9
```

This deal tests your partnership understanding of the meaning of a cuebid of a weak two-bid. Is it asking for a notrump stopper or is it Michaels? If the former, East bids 3♠ and West can't bid 3NT.

Without a stopper the normal procedure with the West hand is to retreat to 4♣ and let East pick the suit. Here, West suspects that East has solid clubs so maybe he has enough outside values to jump to 5♣ instead of just bidding 4♣.

At many tables the opening bid was 3♠ and East simply jumped to 5♣. At our table the auction was exciting. David opened only 2♠ (we play that 3♠ at this vulnerability could be very weak) and Italy's Lorenzo Lauria doubled. I raised to 3♠ and Alfredo Versace made a responsive double. Lauria bid 4♣, forcing (see Deal 10). Versace bid 4♡ and Lauria bid 5♣. Versace pressed on with 5◊ and Lauria bid 6♣! Versace still didn't get the message and tried 6◊. Now, Lauria bid 6♠ to ask his partner to chose between 6NT or 7♣. This might have been brilliant strategy; maybe Versace had K-x of spades. Rather than bid 7♣, Versace did in fact try 6NT. Everyone passed (if I doubled it would have suggested a non-spade lead). Had David led anything but a spade, 6NT could have been made! The run of the clubs would squeeze me in three suits. I must throw the two spades to hold the ♡Kx and ◊KJ10. Then declarer keeps one heart and four diamonds, so he can duck a diamond to me and take the rest. David led the ♠A and I followed low. David continued spades and we beat them only one trick, but won 12 IMPs against the datum of 620.

The other seven pairs played in 5♣, making eleven tricks (two of them were doubled). For playing in clubs presume eleven tricks and lose 1 IMP. If you reached any other game, presume down two (but 3NT is down three — lose 14 IMPs).

Dealer East, Both Vul.
E–W Datum +740

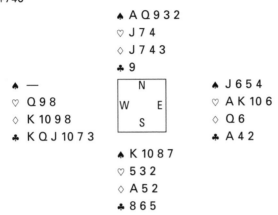

♠ A Q 9 3 2
♥ J 7 4
♦ J 7 4 3
♣ 9

♠ —
♥ Q 9 8
♦ K 10 9 8
♣ K Q J 10 7 3

N
W   E
S

♠ J 6 5 4
♥ A K 10 6
♦ Q 6
♣ A 4 2

♠ K 10 8 7
♥ 5 3 2
♦ A 5 2
♣ 8 6 5

The fit is magical; East-West have just enough to make 6♣ a good contract. On the lie of the cards, presume twelve tricks in clubs, but only seven tricks in notrump. Only one East-West pair fell into the notrump trap, and five of the other seven pairs rested safely in 5♣.

The winning auctions (by Lambardi-Lucena and Mihov-Nanev) began with East opening 1NT (strong!) West transferred to clubs and splintered in spades and East moved toward the slam. The strong club pairs (including us) had difficulty because we started with 1♦, guaranteeing only two diamonds. Now the West hand is barely worth a game force, and, facing a balanced minimum, it's hard to reach the good slam.

The datum was 740, so missing the slam costs only 3 IMPs. Reaching 3NT is a disaster that costs you 14 IMPs, and getting to 6♣ is worth a pickup of 12 big IMPs.

Deal 15

Dealer North, Both Vul.
E–W Datum +460

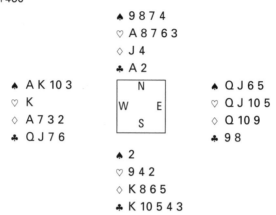

                ♠ 9 8 7 4
                ♡ A 8 7 6 3
                ◇ J 4
                ♣ A 2

    ♠ A K 10 3   ♠ Q J 6 5
    ♡ K   N   ♡ Q J 10 5
    ◇ A 7 3 2   W   E   ◇ Q 10 9
    ♣ Q J 7 6   S   ♣ 9 8

                ♠ 2
                ♡ 9 4 2
                ◇ K 8 6 5
                ♣ K 10 5 4 3

The theme for this tournament seemed to be that 3NT was always better than four of a major in an eight-card fit (see Deals 7, 9 and 11). Many spade declarers were held to nine tricks, but you can presume ten tricks if you reached spades (my gift to you).

Three notrump was much more comfortable with nine easy tricks available. So reaching game meant a small gain, but resting in a partial was costly. My recommended start would be

West	East
	pass
1♣	1♡
1♠	2♠

After this, West should bid notrump (but if he bids only 2NT, East has to guess to raise to game).

Dealer South, Neither Vul.
E–W Datum +530

South opens 4◇
(a good 4♠ opening);
North bids 4♠ if
possible.

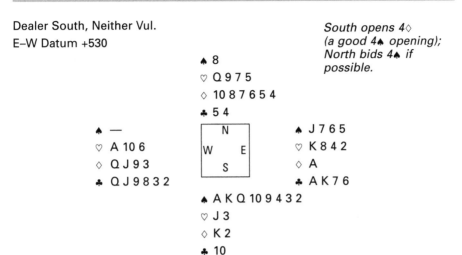

```
                    ♠ 8
                    ♡ Q 9 7 5
                    ◇ 10 8 7 6 5 4
                    ♣ 5 4
    ♠ —                  N          ♠ J 7 6 5
    ♡ A 10 6      W         E       ♡ K 8 4 2
    ◇ Q J 9 3          S           ◇ A
    ♣ Q J 9 8 3 2                  ♣ A K 7 6
                    ♠ A K Q 10 9 4 3 2
                    ♡ J 3
                    ◇ K 2
                    ♣ 10
```

I think I showed poor judgment on this deal. I held the West cards and over South's Namyats 4◇ opening I might have doubled. We conventionally play this double as a light takeout; with a stronger takeout we pass and then double 4♠. This is a safe method because the opponents can't penalize you; they are on their way to 4♠ and if East is in trouble, he can simply leave 4◇ doubled in; they aren't playing there. I passed over 4◇ and then over North's 4♠, David also passed (he might have doubled, but was afraid of hearing 5◇ from me). When North's 4♠ came back to me I think I should have balanced with 5♣. I know it looks good with all the cards in view, but even single dummy it seems right; South probably has all his cards in spades and North didn't have slam interest, so David is marked with some high cards. Over my 5♣ balance David would probably have punished me and raised to 6♣ for 920. In fact, if you guess diamonds, you can make all thirteen tricks, but presume down one if you reached 7♣ (as one pair did).

The datum was 530, so bidding 6♣ is worth 9 IMPs, while getting to the grand costs you 12. Defending 4♠ gets you 100 and a loss of 10 IMPs.

Deal 17

Dealer East, Neither Vul.
E–W Datum +270

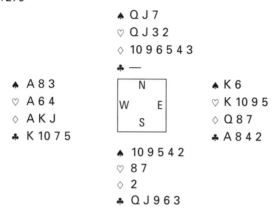

                        ♠ Q J 7
                        ♡ Q J 3 2
                        ◇ 10 9 6 5 4 3
                        ♣ —

    ♠ A 8 3   ┌─────────┐   ♠ K 6
    ♡ A 6 4   │   N   │   ♡ K 10 9 5
    ◇ A K J   │ W   E │   ◇ Q 8 7
    ♣ K 10 7 5   │   S   │   ♣ A 8 4 2
                       └─────────┘
                        ♠ 10 9 5 4 2
                        ♡ 8 7
                        ◇ 2
                        ♣ Q J 9 6 3

How do you stay out of slam when your partner opens the bidding and you have a prime 19-count and a fit? Two of the five pairs that stopped short started with a 10-12 notrump, quietly raised to 3NT. The other three successful pairs started with 1♣ by East, but West simply judged to take the low road. The remaining Wests drove to 6♣, which is a poor contract. With the actual 5-0 club break you can presume down two and -100 if you reach 6♣ (lose 9 IMPs). For notrump contracts presume eleven tricks (lose 8 IMPs for 6NT). The datum was 270, so stopping in game is worth 5 IMPs.

Dealer North, N–S Vul.
E–W Datum +840

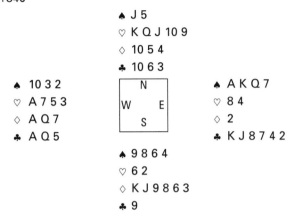

```
                        ♠ J 5
                        ♡ K Q J 10 9
                        ◇ 10 5 4
                        ♣ 10 6 3
   ♠ 10 3 2                              ♠ A K Q 7
   ♡ A 7 5 3          N                  ♡ 8 4
   ◇ A Q 7        W       E              ◇ 2
   ♣ A Q 5            S                  ♣ K J 8 7 4 2
                        ♠ 9 8 6 4
                        ♡ 6 2
                        ◇ K J 9 8 6 3
                        ♣ 9
```

This is a great 6♣. It needs either the diamond finesse or something favorable in spades. As the cards lie thirteen tricks were there, so if you stumbled into 7♣ (as did Chagas–Branco) you win 12 IMPs. For reaching 6♣ you gain only 3 IMPs against the datum of 840. Three pairs bid to 3NT and lost 8 IMPs.

We started with a Precision 2♣ (promising six) and easily reached the slam. After a standard auction such as

West	East
	1♣
1♡	1♠
2◇[1]	3♣

1. Fourth–suit forcing.

West should at least invite a slam, and East has enough to cooperate.

Deal 19

Dealer West, Both Vul.
E–W Datum +490

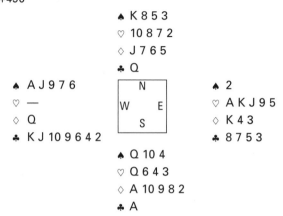

```
                        ♠ K 8 5 3
                        ♡ 10 8 7 2
                        ◊ J 7 6 5
                        ♣ Q
    ♠ A J 9 7 6      ┌─────────┐      ♠ 2
    ♡ —             │    N    │      ♡ A K J 9 5
    ◊ Q             │ W     E │      ◊ K 4 3
    ♣ K J 10 9 6 4 2 │    S    │      ♣ 8 7 5 3
                     └─────────┘
                        ♠ Q 10 4
                        ♡ Q 6 4 3
                        ◊ A 10 9 8 2
                        ♣ A
```

The trick here is to avoid 3NT (or slam!). I suppose you can chalk up a lucky 600 if you reached 3NT by East (South is not likely to lead the ◊A). Two pairs reached the doomed club slam (but it would make on the wrong lead), so the datum was only 490. Chagas–Branco won 11 IMPs for playing in five clubs redoubled (that's 1000 if you're scoring at home).

Score +600 and 3 IMPs for 3NT by East, –100 (–11 IMPs) for 3NT by West, +600 for ♣5 (+3 IMPs) and –100 for 6♣ (–11 IMPs).

Dealer East, Both Vul.
E–W Datum +1670

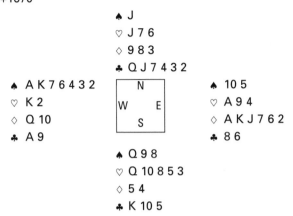

```
                    ♠ J
                    ♡ J 7 6
                    ◇ 9 8 3
                    ♣ Q J 7 4 3 2
     ♠ A K 7 6 4 3 2    ┌─────┐    ♠ 10 5
     ♡ K 2              │  N  │    ♡ A 9 4
     ◇ Q 10          W  │     │  E  ◇ A K J 7 6 2
     ♣ A 9             │  S  │    ♣ 8 6
                       └─────┘
                    ♠ Q 9 8
                    ♡ Q 10 8 5 3
                    ◇ 5 4
                    ♣ K 10 5
```

Only three of the eight pairs reached the laydown grand in diamonds. Seven spades would make if spades were 2–2, but they weren't, so spades makes only twelve tricks. Reaching 6♠ is a 6-IMP loss against the datum of 1670, but that's better than the 18 IMPs that bidding 7♠ costs you. A strong jump shift response of 2♠ would be a good way for West to start after East's 1◇, but most of the field didn't have that available. The standard auction begins

WEST	EAST
	1◇
1♠	2◇

Now West has to make some sort of forcing bid. If he can get a 3◇ bid out of East he can then use Roman Key Card Blackwood in diamonds to go straight to the diamond grand, or maybe he can use Blackwood right over 2◇.

Take 10 IMPs if you got to 7◇, and lose 7 IMPs for stopping in 6◇.

Final standings

Top ten finishers (out of sixteen)

Mahmood–Robson	(USA–UK)	+152
Levin–Weinstein	(USA)	+146
Jassem–Tuszynski	(Poland)	+89
Chagas–Branco	(Brazil)	+64
Hampson–Greco	(USA)	+50
Lambardi–Lucena	(Argentina)	+32
Bertens–Nab	(Netherlands)	+5
Hackett–Hackett	(UK)	-6
Meckstroth–Rodwell	(USA)	-17
Mihov–Nanev	(Bulgaria)	-20

Rating guide

- **Minus 20 IMPs or more**   Brush up your partnership.
- **0 to -20 IMPs**   Well, it was a tough set.
- **0 to +20 IMPs**   Nicely done.
- **Plus 20 IMPs** or more   Do you have partners for the next Spingold?

Scoring table

East-West datums and vulnerabilities

1.	-20	NV	**2.**	+300	V
3.	+220	NV	**4.**	+650	V
5.	+1040	V	**6.**	+690	NV
7.	+130	V	**8.**	+20	V
9.	-20	V	**10.**	+430	NV
11.	+140	V	**12.**	+2210	V
13.	+620	V	**14.**	+740	V
15.	+460	V	**16.**	+530	NV
17.	+270	NV	**18.**	+840	NV
19.	+490	V	**20.**	+1670	V

HANDS TO BID

IMP Table

Difference in Points	IMPS	Difference in Points	IMPS
20–40	1	750–890	13
50–80	2	900–1090	14
90–120	3	1100–1290	15
130–160	4	1300–1490	16
170–210	5	1500–1740	17
220–260	6	1750–1990	18
270–310	7	2000–2240	19
320–360	8	2250–2490	20
370–420	9	2500–2990	21
430–490	10	3000–3490	22
500–590	11	3500–3990	23
600–740	12	4000–and up	24

1. ♠ K J 8 7   *Dealer South,*
♡ A Q 4   *E-W Vul.*
◊ A 10 6
♣ Q 10 3

South passes, but later enters with a diamond bid at any level.

2. ♠ K J 10   *Dealer West,*
♡ A 10 6 5   *Both Vul.*
◊ A K 9 7 3
♣ A

3. ♠ —   *Dealer East,*
♡ J 7 5 3   *N-S Vul.*
◊ K J 9 6
♣ Q 10 6 3 2

4. ♠ J 8   *Dealer North,*
♡ A 10 9 8 4   *E-W Vul.*
◊ A K Q 8 7
♣ 10

5. ♠ A J 7 5 4   *Dealer West,*
♡ 8 6 4   *Neither Vul.*
◊ A J 4
♣ J 6

6. ♠ 6 5 2   *Dealer North,*
♡ 10 9 7 5 3   *E-W Vul.*
◊ A 7 5
♣ A Q

7. ♠ K 5   *Dealer South,*
♡ K Q J 6   *E-W Vul.*
◊ K 9 6 2
♣ 9 6 4

8. ♠ 9 4 2   *Dealer West,*
♡ 9   *Neither Vul.*
◊ K Q J 9 3 2
♣ 10 9 4

9. ♠ K   *Dealer North,*
♡ A Q 9   *E-W Vul.*
◊ A Q 9 8 5
♣ Q 10 7 4

10. ♠ A Q 10 2   *Dealer East,*
♡ J 4   *Both Vul.*
◊ K 5 4 3
♣ K J 3

South overcalls in hearts, and North jump-raises hearts, skipping a level.

11. ♠ K   *Dealer North,*
♡ A 8 6   *Neither Vul.*
◊ J 8 7 6 5 4
♣ A K 3

South bids hearts and North raises one level.

12. ♠ Q 5   *Dealer South,*
♡ —   *Both Vul.*
◊ A Q 9 8 5 4 2
♣ A K J 3

13. ♠ A 10 9 7 2   *Dealer South,*
♡ —   *Neither Vul.*
◊ K J 10 6 4 3 2
♣ 7

South opens 3♡.

14. ♠ K 6 4 2   *Dealer North,*
♡ A 7   *Both Vul.*
◊ A 7 6
♣ K Q 8 4

15. ♠ K Q 8 4 3   *Dealer North,*
♡ 7 4 2   *Neither Vul.*
◊ A Q
♣ K 7 5

North opens 2♡.

16. ♠ 5   *Dealer East,*
♡ A 8 5 3   *E-W Vul.*
◊ 3
♣ A K J 7 6 5 2

17. ♠ A Q J 7 5 3   *Dealer East,*
♡ —   *Neither Vul.*
◊ 8 6 5 4
♣ 7 6 4

South overcalls in hearts and North raises one level.

18. ♠ A 8 6 3   *Dealer North,*
♡ Q 10 5   *Both Vul.*
◊ K 9 4
♣ 9 7 4

19. ♠ A Q 6   *Dealer South,*
♡ 5 3   *N-S Vul.*
◊ A
♣ A K 10 9 8 7 4

North overcalls in hearts.

20. ♠ K Q 6   *Dealer West,*
♡ A J 8   *Both Vul.*
◊ K 10 3
♣ J 10 8 7

1. ♠ K 8 7   *Dealer West,*
     ♡ A K Q 9 8 6 4   *Both Vul.*
     ◇ 4
     ♣ A J

South bids diamonds.

2. ♠ 4   *Dealer West,*
     ♡ K 10 7   *N-S Vul.*
     ◇ 9 8 5 4
     ♣ A K 7 6 3

3. ♠ A 9 8 4 2   *Dealer East,*
     ♡ J 5   *Both Vul.*
     ◇ A 2
     ♣ J 8 6 4

4. ♠ A K 4 3   *Dealer West,*
     ♡ A 10 9 8 5   *N-S Vul.*
     ◇ Q 5
     ♣ K 10

5. ♠ J 10   *Dealer North,*
     ♡ 6 3   *Both Vul.*
     ◇ K J 10 7 6 4 3 2
     ♣ 2

South bids spades, North bids 3♠ and South bids 4♠.

6. ♠ A 6   *Dealer South,*
     ♡ J 8 5 3   *Both Vul.*
     ◇ A K Q 10 8 6
     ♣ 8

7. ♠ J 5 4   *Dealer West,*
     ♡ 8 6 3 2   *E-W Vul.*
     ◇ A 3
     ♣ K Q J 3

South bids 2♡, North bids 4♡.

8. ♠ 8 5 3   *Dealer South,*
     ♡ A K J 10 9 2   *Both Vul.*
     ◇ 7
     ♣ K J 5

South opens 1◇.

9. ♠ 7   *Dealer South,*
     ♡ A J 10 9   *Neither Vul.*
     ◇ K 9 6 3 2
     ♣ K 9 8

South passes, then bids spades. North bids 4♠.

10. ♠ J 4 2   *Dealer West,*
     ♡ —   *Neither Vul.*
     ◇ A K Q 9 8 6 4
     ♣ Q J 5

11. ♠ 7 6   *Dealer West,*
     ♡ A K   *N-S Vul.*
     ◇ A K Q 9 5
     ♣ A J 10 3

12. ♠ 7 6   *Dealer East,*
     ♡ K 10 9 5 3   *N-S Vul.*
     ◇ A 10 9 8 6 4
     ♣ —

13. ♠ 9 8 3   *Dealer West,*
     ♡ 3   *Both Vul.*
     ◇ 5 3 2
     ♣ A Q 10 9 7 3

14. ♠ K 10 7 6   *Dealer North,*
     ♡ A 9 2   *Both Vul.*
     ◇ A K 10 9 2
     ♣ 4

15. ♠ A J 10 7   *Dealer North,*
     ♡ K Q 10 7 4 2   *Neither Vul.*
     ◇ 10
     ♣ A 6

1. ♠ J 10 7 5 4 — *Dealer West,*
♡ A Q — *Both Vul.*
◇ 10
♣ A K 5 4 3

2. ♠ A Q J 5 — *Dealer West,*
♡ A 6 — *Both Vul.*
◇ A 4 3
♣ Q 6 4 3

3. ♠ J 9 7 — *Dealer East,*
♡ A — *E-W Vul.*
◇ A K 9 8 6
♣ A 10 8 7

West bids spades at the minimum level.

4. ♠ K 10 3 — *Dealer East,*
♡ A 6 — *E-W Vul.*
◇ A J 10 5 3 2
♣ Q 10

5. ♠ 9 6 4 — *Dealer South,*
♡ A K — *N-S Vul.*
◇ K 6 4
♣ A 7 5 3 2

6. ♠ K 10 — *Dealer North,*
♡ K 9 6 4 2 — *Both Vul.*
◇ K 6 4 3
♣ 6 3

7. ♠ Q 10 8 4 — *Dealer West,*
♡ 9 3 — *Both Vul.*
◇ K 10 9
♣ J 10 9 7

East bids spades at the minimum level.

8. ♠ Q 7 6 3 — *Dealer North,*
♡ 9 — *Neither Vul.*
◇ K J 6 5 4 2
♣ A J

9. ♠ J 10 4 — *Dealer North,*
♡ Q J 10 — *E-W Vul.*
◇ A Q 10 9 7 5
♣ 10

10. ♠ A K 8 3 2 — *Dealer East,*
♡ 2 — *Both Vul.*
◇ J 10 5 4
♣ A 5 3

11. ♠ A Q J 10 4 2 — *Dealer East,*
♡ 4 — *Neither Vul.*
◇ Q 4
♣ A K J 6

12. ♠ K 6 — *Dealer East,*
♡ K Q — *E-W Vul.*
◇ A J 9 8 5 4
♣ 8 5 3

13. ♠ K 10 9 5 — *Dealer South,*
♡ — — *Both Vul.*
◇ 10 9 6 4 3
♣ K J 8 2

West bids hearts at the minimum level and East single jump-raises hearts.

14. ♠ K 10 9 — *Dealer East,*
♡ 9 8 7 — *E-W Vul.*
◇ 7 4
♣ A 9 7 4 3

East deals and opens 1◇, West passes.

15. ♠ A 7 — *Dealer North,*
♡ A J 8 3 — *E-W Vul.*
◇ K 10
♣ Q J 7 6 4

16. ♠ 7 2 — *Dealer East,*
♡ J 7 6 — *N-S Vul.*
◇ A Q
♣ K Q J 7 3 2

17. ♠ J 8 7 6 4 2 — *Dealer North,*
♡ A Q 7 6 — *Neither Vul.*
◇ —
♣ Q 8 2

18. ♠ A 5 4 3 — *Dealer South,*
♡ 9 — *Neither Vul.*
◇ A K Q 2
♣ Q J 7 6

West cuebids if possible to show majors, and East bids 2♡ if possible at his first turn.

19. ♠ 8 4 2 — *Dealer South,*
♡ A 9 — *Both Vul.*
◇ A K Q 8 7 6 4
♣ 8

20. ♠ A 10 — *Dealer West,*
♡ K 10 8 4 — *N-S Vul.*
◇ K 9 8 6 5 2
♣ 7

1. ♠ J 10 8 4   *Dealer West,*
   ♡ A 9 3   *N-S Vul.*
   ◇ 7
   ♣ A K J 8 4

   West opens 2◇, East bids 3◇.

2. ♠ A J 3   *Dealer South,*
   ♡ Q 8 7 3   *Neither Vul.*
   ◇ K 5 4
   ♣ Q 6 5

3. ♠ A 10 8 5 2   *Dealer South,*
   ♡ —   *N-S Vul.*
   ◇ A K 10 5
   ♣ A Q 9 5

   East overcalls 1♡ if possible, after which West jump-raises hearts.

4. ♠ K 10   *Dealer North,*
   ♡ A K J   *E-W Vul.*
   ◇ A J 6
   ♣ K Q J 9 6

5. ♠ A Q 10 6 3   *Dealer East,*
   ♡ K 5 3   *N-S Vul.*
   ◇ A
   ♣ A Q 10 6

6. ♠ K 5 4 2   *Dealer South,*
   ♡ 10   *N-S Vul.*
   ◇ K Q 7 2
   ♣ A J 8 6

   West bids 1♠ if possible.

7. ♠ J 9 5   *Dealer East,*
   ♡ J 6   *N-S Vul.*
   ◇ A K 7 3
   ♣ K 10 7 6

8. ♠ A K 7 6   *Dealer West,*
   ♡ K Q 8 6 5 3   *Both Vul.*
   ◇ 8
   ♣ J 5

9. ♠ 10   *Dealer East,*
   ♡ A K 10 5   *E-W Vul.*
   ◇ A K 8 6 5
   ♣ K Q 4

10. ♠ 4   *Dealer East,*
    ♡ J 8 2   *Both Vul.*
    ◇ Q 7 5 3
    ♣ K J 9 7 4

11. ♠ A J   *Dealer North,*
    ♡ A Q 10 6   *Neither Vul.*
    ◇ A J 6 4
    ♣ K 10 3

12 ♠ A J 7 2   *Dealer South,*
    ♡ K 10 7 6 5   *E-W Vul.*
    ◇ J 4
    ♣ A 10

13. ♠ K Q   *Dealer East,*
    ♡ K 10 6 5   *Both Vul.*
    ◇ K 2
    ♣ A K Q 10 2

14. ♠ K J 8   *Dealer West,*
    ♡ A K J 9   *N-S Vul.*
    ◇ Q 10 9 2
    ♣ 10 5

15. ♠ —   *Dealer South,*
    ♡ K 8 5 2   *Neither Vul.*
    ◇ A 9 8 7 6 4 3
    ♣ 6 4

    East bids 2♠, West raises spades one level.

16. ♠ K Q 4 3   *Dealer North,*
    ♡ J 7 5 3   *Neither Vul.*
    ◇ K 7
    ♣ Q 8 3

17. ♠ A K J 9   *Dealer North,*
    ♡ A J 10 7 4   *Both Vul.*
    ◇ K Q 4
    ♣ Q

    If possible, East opens 2♣ (natural, 11-15). West raises to 3♣.

18. ♠ J 9 6 5   *Dealer South,*
    ♡ A 9 8 5   *N-S Vul.*
    ◇ J 5 4 3 2
    ♣ —

    West opens 1♣.

19. ♠ K Q 8 2   *Dealer South,*
    ♡ A 10 7 4   *Both Vul.*
    ◇ K J 9 3
    ♣ 8

20. ♠ Q 6 4   *Dealer East,*
    ♡ K Q 2   *Both Vul.*
    ◇ A 9
    ♣ K Q J 8 2

    East opens 3◇.

1.
♠ 9 3　　　*Dealer West,*
♡ K 8　　　*Both Vul.*
◊ A K Q J 4
♣ A Q J 8

East bids 1♠.

2.
♠ 8 4 2　　　*Dealer East,*
♡ Q J 8 7 6 4　　*Both Vul.*
◊ 6 5 2
♣ J

3.
♠ K J 9 5　　　*Dealer East,*
♡ Q 7 5 3　　　*N-S Vul.*
◊ K 8 5
♣ A 5

*West bids 1♡ if possible, and East raises hearts
one level.*

4.
♠ A 8 6 5　　　*Dealer West,*
♡ 2　　　　　*Both Vul.*
◊ A K 7 5 4 2
♣ 6 5

*West opens 2♡ (0-11 HCP, at least nine cards in
the majors, 5-4 either way); East passes.*

5.
♠ 7　　　　　*Dealer West,*
♡ K Q 10 9 7 5 2　*N-S Vul.*
◊ 10
♣ A 10 5 3

*East overcalls 1♠ if possible, and, if he does,
West raises to 5♠!*

6.
♠ A 9 8　　　*Dealer West,*
♡ A 10 7　　　*Both Vul.*
◊ —
♣ K Q J 6 4 3 2

7.
♠ 9 6 3　　　*Dealer East,*
♡ J 9 8 2　　　*Both Vul.*
◊ K 2
♣ A K Q 2

East opens 1◊, West raises to 2◊.

8.
♠ Q 10 4　　　*Dealer East,*
♡ Q 9 5　　　*Both Vul.*
◊ A Q
♣ A K J 8 3

9.
♠ K J 9　　　*Dealer West,*
♡ A Q 9 8 4　　*Neither Vul.*
◊ K 4
♣ K Q 4

10.
♠ K Q J 8 6 4　*Dealer North,*
♡ Q 4 2　　　*Both Vul.*
◊ K Q 8 3
♣ —

11.
♠ 4　　　　　*Dealer East,*
♡ A K Q 7 6 3　*N-S Vul.*
◊ 10 7 6
♣ A K Q

East opens 3♠, West bids 4♠.

12.
♠ Q J　　　　*Dealer East,*
♡ K 6 2　　　*N-S Vul.*
◊ A Q 10 8 5 2
♣ K 9

East opens 2♡.

13.
♠ K 10 3 2　　*Dealer North,*
♡ —　　　　　*Neither Vul.*
◊ A K 9 4 2
♣ K Q J 2

14.
♠ 4 2　　　　*Dealer South,*
♡ A J 10 9 7　*E-W Vul.*
◊ J 6
♣ K Q 7 6

15.
♠ K 6 5　　　*Dealer East,*
♡ J 10 3　　　*Neither Vul.*
◊ A
♣ A K Q J 6 4

16.
♠ A J 10　　　*Dealer North,*
♡ 9 6　　　　*E-W Vul.*
◊ 7 4 3 2
♣ Q 5 4 2

17.
♠ A Q 7 5 3 2　*Dealer West,*
♡ A 8　　　　*N-S Vul.*
◊ 4
♣ K 10 8 5

West opens 3◊.

18.
♠ A 10 3　　　*Dealer West,*
♡ K 6 4　　　*Neither Vul.*
◊ J 10 9 2
♣ K Q 5

*East bids spades, West raises to 3♠ if possible; if
it's a jump, it's weak.*

19.
♠ 4　　　　　*Dealer East,*
♡ A 6 5 2　　*N-S Vul.*
◊ J 8 7 6 4
♣ Q 10 9

East opens 3♠, West bids 4♠.

20.
♠ Q 10 7 5　　*Dealer West,*
♡ J 9 2　　　*Both Vul.*
◊ K 6 5
♣ K 9 6

*East bids 2◊; if North opens 1NT, 2◊ = ◊ + a
major.　If South doubles, it goes redouble
(rescue), pass, pass.*

Hands to Bid • 163

1
♠ K 9 7   *Dealer East,*
♡ A J 9 8 2   *N-S Vul.*
◇ K 7 3 2
♣ 7

2.
♠ K 6   *Dealer South,*
♡ A K 9 8 4   *N-S Vul.*
◇ A J 10
♣ A K 8

3.
♠ A K 4   *Dealer East,*
♡ A 10 9   *N-S Vul.*
◇ A Q J 7 5
♣ 6 5

East opens 1♡, West bids clubs and East bids 5♣.

4.
♠ 6   *Dealer West,*
♡ 4   *Both Vul.*
◇ 8 7 5 3 2
♣ A K J 8 5 3

East bids spades and West raises if below 4♠ level.

5.
♠ A 8   *Dealer North,*
♡ 10 9 8   *Both Vul.*
◇ A K 10 2
♣ K 8 5 3

East opens 1♣ (if possible), West responds 1♠, and East bids 2♠

6.
♠ A Q 5 4   *Dealer South,*
♡ 5 4 3   *Both Vul.*
◇ K Q 10
♣ Q 8 5

7.
♠ K Q 10 9 7   *Dealer West,*
♡ A 9 7 6   *Neither Vul.*
◇ A
♣ 7 6 4

8.
♠ 10 2   *Dealer West,*
♡ A K J 8 2   *N-S Vul.*
◇ A 10 8 6 5
♣ 3

West opens 3♠, East bids 4♠ if possible.

9.
♠ Q 3   *Dealer West,*
♡ A K J 7 5 2   *E-W Vul.*
◇ A 10 9 7
♣ 9

10.
♠ Q 4   *Dealer North,*
♡ Q 6   *E-W Vul.*
◇ J 6 5 4 3 2
♣ A K 4

11.
♠ K 6 5 3   *Dealer South,*
♡ K J 9   *E-W Vul.*
◇ A Q J 10 8
♣ 5

12.
♠ A 6   *Dealer North,*
♡ K Q 9 6 3   *Neither Vul.*
◇ A K 6
♣ 10 8 7

13.
♠ 4   *Dealer East,*
♡ K 8 4   *N-S Vul.*
◇ A 9 8 2
♣ A Q 8 6 4

14.
♠ A K   *Dealer South,*
♡ A Q 9 7 4 2   *N-S Vul.*
◇ Q J 5
♣ Q J

15.
♠ A Q 4   *Dealer East,*
♡ A K Q J 6 5   *N-S Vul.*
◇ A 8
♣ 8 5

West bids 2♠.

16.
♠ 4   *Dealer North,*
♡ K Q 10 8   *Both Vul.*
◇ 7
♣ A Q 8 7 6 5 3

East bids diamonds, West bids minimum number of spades (not forcing).

17.
♠ Q 8 7   *Dealer East,*
♡ J 8 6   *E-W Vul.*
◇ 8 5
♣ A K J 10 6

18.
♠ 9 7 3   *Dealer East,*
♡ A 4   *Both Vul.*
◇ A K 7
♣ A Q J 7 6

West bids 1♡ if possible

19.
♠ 7   *Dealer East,*
♡ K Q 10 8 7 6 5   *Neither Vul.*
◇ 8 7
♣ Q J 2

West	North	East	South
		pass	1♠
3♡	3NT	4♡	4NT
pass	6◇	pass	6NT
pass	pass	dbl	7♠
all pass			

What is your opening lead as West?

20.
♠ A Q 5   *Dealer South,*
♡ J 5   *N-S Vul.*
◇ 10 8 5 3
♣ K 6 4 3

West	North	East	South
			3♠
pass	4♠	dbl	all pass

What is your opening lead as West?

1. ♠ 9 3   *Dealer North,*
♡ A 7 2   *N-S Vul.*
♢ 4
♣ A 10 8 6 5 3 2

North opens 1♠. South bids 1NT if possible,
North bids 2♢ if possible and South raises to
3♢ if possible.

2. ♠ A Q J   *Dealer East,*
♡ K Q 9 7 5 2   *E-W Vul.*
♢ A 9 6
♣ 10

South opens 1♣.

3. ♠ J 4   *Dealer East,*
♡ K 7 4   *N-S Vul.*
♢ A 8 4 2
♣ Q J 10 4

South bids 1♠.

4. ♠ A Q 2   *Dealer East,*
♡ J 9 6 3   *Both Vul.*
♢ K Q 10
♣ A 9 4

5. ♠ Q 9 2   *Dealer North,*
♡ J 7   *Both Vul.*
♢ A 3
♣ A Q J 10 3 2

6. ♠ A J 6 4 3 2   *Dealer East,*
♡ 8 3   *Neither Vul.*
♢ A K Q 2
♣ A

7. ♠ A Q J 10   *Dealer East,*
♡ A 5   *E-W Vul.*
♢ 10 9 2
♣ J 9 3 2

8. ♠ K J 4 3   *Dealer North,*
♡ 8   *E-W Vul.*
♢ A J 8 2
♣ 8 7 4 2

North opens 3♡.

9. ♠ K 8 3   *Dealer East,*
♡ A Q 7 6 4 3   *Both Vul.*
♢ A 7 3
♣ 5

10. ♠ A 6 5 2   *Dealer South,*
♡ 4   *N-S Vul.*
♢ A J 10 7 6 5
♣ K Q

South opens 2♡ and North bids 3♡.

11. ♠ 8 6 4 3   *West dealer,*
♡ A J 5 4 2   *Both Vul.*
♢ 4
♣ A Q J

North bids 2♢.

12. ♠ A 10 3   *Dealer North,*
♡ Q 3 2   *E-W Vul.*
♢ K J 8 7 6
♣ A K

13. ♠ J 10   *Dealer North,*
♡ Q 10 9 8 5   *E-W Vul.*
♢ A Q 9 5 4
♣ 6

North opens 2♠.

14. ♠ —   *Dealer East,*
♡ Q 9 8   *Both Vul.*
♢ K 10 9 8
♣ K Q J 10 7 3

15. ♠ A K 10 3   *Dealer North,*
♡ K   *Both Vul.*
♢ A 7 3 2
♣ Q J 7 6

16. ♠ —   *Dealer South,*
♡ A 10 6   *Neither Vul.*
♢ Q J 9 3
♣ Q J 9 8 3 2

South opens 4♢ showing a good 4♠ opening;
North bids 4♠ if possible.

17. ♠ A 8 3   *Dealer East,*
♡ A 6 4   *Neither Vul.*
♢ A K J
♣ K 10 7 5

18. ♠ 10 3 2   *Dealer North,*
♡ A 7 5 3   *N-S Vul.*
♢ A Q 7
♣ A Q 5

19. ♠ A J 9 7 6   *Dealer West,*
♡ —   *Both Vul.*
♢ Q
♣ K J 10 9 6 4 2

20. ♠ A K 7 6 4 3 2 *Dealer East,*
♡ K 2   *Both Vul.*
♢ Q 10
♣ A 9

1.
♠ Q
♥ K J 6
♦ 7
♣ A K J 9 8 7 4 2

Dealer South,
E-W Vul.

South passes, but later enters with a diamond bid at any level.

2.
♠ A 7 6 3
♥ Q J 9 7 4
♦ 8 4
♣ Q 8

Dealer West,
Both Vul.

3.
♠ A 8 5
♥ A Q
♦ A 8 5 4 3 2
♣ A 7

Dealer East,
N-S Vul.

4.
♠ A
♥ K Q
♦ 10 4 3 2
♣ A J 9 8 7 3

Dealer North,
E-W Vul.

5.
♠ K Q 6 3
♥ K Q J 5
♦ K
♣ A 10 8 3

Dealer West,
Neither Vul.

6.
♠ A Q J 3
♥ K Q 2
♦ K 10 9
♣ 9 5 3

Dealer North,
E-W Vul.

7.
♠ A 4 3
♥ 2
♦ A 10 5 4
♣ A K J 7 3

Dealer South,
E-W Vul.

8.
♠ A 8
♥ A J 7 4 3 2
♦ 8 6
♣ A K Q

Dealer West,
Neither Vul.

9.
♠ A Q 8 5 3
♥ K 8
♦ J 7 6 4
♣ A K

Dealer North,
E-W Vul.

10.
♠ K 8 6 5
♥ —
♦ A 8 2
♣ A Q 6 5 4 2

Dealer East,
Both Vul.

South overcalls in hearts, and North jump-raises hearts, skipping a level.

11.
♠ 10 9 5 3 2
♥ 10 3
♦ A K Q 10 3
♣ 2

Dealer North,
Neither Vul.

South bids hearts and North raises one level.

12.
♠ A K 9 7 2
♥ K 8 3
♦ 6
♣ Q 5 4 2

Dealer South,
Both Vul.

13.
♠ 3
♥ K Q 9
♦ A Q 9
♣ A K Q J 6 4

Dealer South,
Neither Vul.

South opens 3♥.

14.
♠ A Q J 5
♥ K Q 10 8 4 3
♦ 9
♣ A 6

Dealer North,
Both Vul.

15.
♠ A 10 2
♥ A
♦ K 9 7 6 3
♣ A 9 6 3

Dealer North,
Neither Vul.

North opens 2♥.

16.
♠ K Q J 10 9 3
♥ 7 2
♦ K 6 4 2
♣ 8

Dealer East,
E-W Vul.

17.
♠ K 10 9
♥ 10 9 3
♦ A K J 7
♣ A J 3

Dealer East,
Neither Vul.

South overcalls in hearts and North raises one level.

18.
♠ K Q 7 5
♥ K 7 4 2
♦ A Q 8
♣ K 3

Dealer North,
Both Vul.

19.
♠ K 9
♥ J 4 2
♦ K 10 3 2
♣ Q J 6 3

Dealer South,
N-S Vul.

North overcalls in hearts.

20.
♠ A 10 5 2
♥ K 7
♦ A Q 6
♣ A 6 5 3

Dealer West,
Both Vul.

1.　♠ Q J 10 2　　*Dealer West,*
　　　　♡ 5 2　　　　　*Both Vul.*
　　　　◇ A K 9
　　　　♣ K 7 6 3
South bids diamonds

2.　♠ A 7　　　　*Dealer West,*
　　　　♡ A Q J　　　*N-S Vul.*
　　　　◇ A K Q 10 7
　　　　♣ 10 4 2

3.　♠ K Q 6 3　　*Dealer East,*
　　　　♡ A K 6　　　*Both Vul.*
　　　　◇ K 10 6 5
　　　　♣ K Q

4.　♠ Q 9 8 2　　*Dealer West,*
　　　　♡ K 4 3　　　*N-S Vul.*
　　　　◇ A J
　　　　♣ A 8 6 3

5.　♠ A 7　　　　*Dealer North,*
　　　　♡ A Q J 7 5　*Both Vul.*
　　　　◇ A 5
　　　　♣ A 8 6 3
South bids spades, North bids 3♠ and South
bids 4♠.

6.　♠ Q 9 8 5　　*Dealer South,*
　　　　♡ A K　　　　*Both Vul.*
　　　　◇ 7 5 4 3
　　　　♣ A 3 2

7.　♠ K Q 8 3　　*Dealer West,*
　　　　♡ —　　　　　*E-W Vul.*
　　　　◇ K Q 10 9 8
　　　　♣ A 10 7 2
South bids 2♡, North bids 4♡.

8.　♠ A J 4　　　*Dealer South,*
　　　　♡ 7 6 4 3　　*Both Vul.*
　　　　◇ K 8 5
　　　　♣ A 10 2
South opens 1◇.

9.　♠ 8 5 4　　　*Dealer South,*
　　　　♡ K Q　　　　*Neither Vul.*
　　　　◇ A Q J 8 7
　　　　♣ A 5 3
South passes, then bids spades. North bids 4♠.

10.　♠ Q 6　　　　*Dealer West,*
　　　　♡ A 9　　　　*Neither Vul.*
　　　　◇ 7 5
　　　　♣ A K 10 9 8 4 3

11.　♠ Q　　　　　*Dealer West,*
　　　　♡ Q J 10 8 7 6 3　*N-S Vul.*
　　　　◇ 8 6 3
　　　　♣ Q 5

12.　♠ A K 2　　　*Dealer East,*
　　　　♡ Q J 8　　　*N-S Vul.*
　　　　◇ K 2
　　　　♣ A 9 6 4 3

13.　♠ A K 10　　*Dealer West,*
　　　　♡ A 9 5　　　*Both Vul.*
　　　　◇ A K 9 8 4
　　　　♣ J 5

14.　♠ A 5　　　　*Dealer North,*
　　　　♡ K J　　　　*Both Vul.*
　　　　◇ Q J 7 5
　　　　♣ A J 10 8 3

15.　♠ Q 6 3　　　*Dealer North,*
　　　　♡ A　　　　　*Neither Vul.*
　　　　◇ A 8 6 5
　　　　♣ K Q 7 5 4

1.
♠ A
♡ 3
◇ A J 9 6 5 2
♣ Q 10 9 8 7
Dealer West,
Both Vul.

2.
♠ —
♡ K J 9 8 7 5
◇ K Q J 10 9 8
♣ J
Dealer West,
Both Vul.

3.
♠ A 10 5 2
♡ K 3
◇ Q J 10 7 2
♣ 6 4
Dealer East,
E-W Vul.

West bids spades at the minimum level.

4.
♠ A
♡ J 10 8 7 2
◇ K Q 6
♣ A J 5 3
Dealer East,
E-W Vul.

5.
♠ J 8
♡ Q 10 2
◇ A 10 9
♣ K Q J 9 8
Dealer South,
N-S Vul.

6.
♠ A 5 4
♡ A Q 5
◇ A J 7 2
♣ J 10 7
Dealer North,
Both Vul.

7.
♠ 9
♡ A Q J 7 6 5
◇ A 7 6
♣ K Q 8
Dealer West,
Both Vul.

East bids spades at the minimum level.

8.
♠ K
♡ A Q J 8 3
◇ A Q 9 3
♣ Q 7 4
Dealer North,
Neither Vul.

9.
♠ A 7 6
♡ A K
◇ —
♣ K Q J 8 7 6 5 4
Dealer North,
E-W Vul.

10.
♠ 10
♡ K 10 7
◇ A K 7 3 2
♣ K 10 7 6
Dealer East,
Both Vul.

11.
♠ 6
♡ A K 10 7 3
◇ A K 8 6 2
♣ 10 3
Dealer East,
Neither Vul.

12.
♠ A J 2
♡ J 9
◇ K 7
♣ A K Q J 9 7
Dealer East,
E-W Vul.

13.
♠ A 2
♡ Q 10 6 5
◇ A
♣ A 10 7 6 5 4
Dealer South,
Both Vul.

West bids hearts at the minimum level and East single jump-raises hearts.

14.
♠ —
♡ K Q
◇ A K Q 5 2
♣ K Q J 8 6 5
Dealer East,
E-W Vul.

East deals and opens 1◇, West passes.

15.
♠ Q 6 4
♡ K
◇ A Q 9 7 5 4
♣ A 5 3
Dealer North,
E-W Vul.

16.
♠ 6 5 4 3
♡ A 8 3
◇ K 9 8 6 4
♣ A
Dealer East,
N-S Vul.

17.
♠ A K 9 5
♡ 10 9 3
◇ A K 5 4
♣ K J
Dealer North,
Neither Vul.

18.
♠ J
♡ A Q J 7
◇ J 9 8 4
♣ 10 8 4 2
Dealer South,
Neither Vul.

West cuebids if possible to show majors, and East bids 2♡ if possible at his first turn.

19.
♠ 10 7 6
♡ K J 10 7
◇ J 2
♣ A K 6 5
Dealer South,
Both Vul.

20.
♠ K 9 7 6
♡ A Q J
◇ A 4 3
♣ Q 5 3
Dealer West,
N-S Vul.

1.   ♠ A K 9 2   *Dealer West,*
     ♡ K Q 6   *N-S Vul.*
     ◇ K 10 6
     ♣ 6 5 2

West opens 2◇, East bids 3◇.

2.   ♠ 10 9 8   *Dealer South,*
     ♡ A K J 6   *Neither Vul.*
     ◇ A Q 7
     ♣ A 3 2

3.   ♠ Q 9 7 4 3   *Dealer South,*
     ♡ 9 7 6 4 3   *N-S Vul.*
     ◇ Q 3
     ♣ 7

East overcalls 1♡ if possible, after which West jump-raises hearts.

4.   ♠ A Q 9 7 6   *Dealer North,*
     ♡ 7 3   *E-W Vul.*
     ◇ K 10 9 7
     ♣ 7 5

5.   ♠ K 9 8   *Dealer East,*
     ♡ A J 9 8 6   *N-S Vul.*
     ◇ 9 8 7
     ♣ K 7

6.   ♠ 7   *Dealer South,*
     ♡ A Q 9 6 4   *N-S Vul.*
     ◇ A 9
     ♣ K Q 9 7 5

West bids 1♠ if possible.

7.   ♠ K Q   *Dealer East,*
     ♡ A K 10 9 4 *N-S Vul.*
     ◇ Q
     ♣ A 9 8 4 3

8.   ♠ Q 4 3   *Dealer West,*
     ♡ A 9   *Both Vul.*
     ◇ A 7 4
     ♣ A Q 10 6 2

9.   ♠ A K 5 4   *Dealer East,*
     ♡ Q 8 7 6   *E-W Vul.*
     ◇ Q J 2
     ♣ 10 2

10. ♠ A K 5   *Dealer East,*
     ♡ A K 6   *Both Vul.*
     ◇ A 9 6 4
     ♣ 6 5 2

11. ♠ K Q 10   *Dealer North,*
     ♡ J 8 7 3   *Neither Vul.*
     ◇ 10 3 2
     ♣ A Q J

12. ♠ Q 10   *Dealer South,*
     ♡ 8 3 2   *E-W Vul.*
     ◇ A K Q 9 3 2
     ♣ Q 5

13. ♠ A 6 5   *Dealer East,*
     ♡ A 9 4 3   *Both Vul.*
     ◇ Q 10 7 5 3
     ♣ 3

14. ♠ A 9 6 5 4   *Dealer West,*
     ♡ 2   *N-S Vul.*
     ◇ A 4
     ♣ A K Q 9 3

15. ♠ 10 8 2   *Dealer South,*
     ♡ A   *Neither Vul.*
     ◇ Q J 5
     ♣ A Q 10 9 7 5

East bids 2♠, West raises spades one level.

16. ♠ A J 10 9 6 2 *Dealer North,*
     ♡ 8 2   *Neither Vul.*
     ◇ 6
     ♣ K J 7 4

17. ♠ Q 8 7   *Dealer North,*
     ♡ 9 8 5   *Both Vul.*
     ◇ A J 10 7 5
     ♣ 9 6

If possible, East opens 2♣ (natural, 11-15). West raises to 3♣.

18. ♠ 4 2   *Dealer South,*
     ♡ J 6 4   *N-S Vul.*
     ◇ K Q 10
     ♣ A K Q 8 6

West opens 1♣.

19. ♠ 9 4   *Dealer South,*
     ♡ K Q J 5 2   *Both Vul.*
     ◇ A 10 6
     ♣ K J 2

20. ♠ 10 9 2   *Dealer East,*
     ♡ A J 4 3   *Both Vul.*
     ◇ Q 3
     ♣ 10 9 7 6

East opens 3◇.

1.
♠ A J 2
♡ 9 7 6 5
◇ 8
♣ 7 6 4 3 2

Dealer West,
Both Vul.

East bids 1♠.

2.
♠ A 5
♡ A K
◇ K Q 3
♣ A K 6 5 3 2

Dealer East,
Both Vul.

3.
♠ A 8 6 4 3 2
♡ 10
◇ Q 9
♣ 10 7 6 3

Dealer East,
N-S Vul.

West bids 1♡ if possible, and East raises hearts one level.

4.
♠ J 2
♡ A Q J 7 5
◇ Q J 9 6
♣ 3 2

Dealer West,
Both Vul.

West opens 2♡ showing 0-11 HCP and at least nine cards in the majors, 5-4 either way; East passes.

5.
♠ Q 4
♡ A 8 6 3
◇ A Q 4 3
♣ K Q 9

Dealer West,
N-S Vul.

East overcalls 1♠ if possible, and, if he does, West raises to 5♠!

6.
♠ Q J 10 7
♡ Q 9 8 6 3
◇ A Q 10 4
♣ —

Dealer West,
Both Vul.

7.
♠ A K Q
♡ 7 6
◇ Q 5 4
♣ J 8 7 6 4

Dealer East,
Both Vul.

East opens 1◇, West raises 2◇.

8.
♠ K J 9 5
♡ A 8 6 3 2
◇ 7
♣ Q 7 4

Dealer East,
Both Vul.

9.
♠ A Q 7
♡ 6 5 3
◇ Q 7
♣ A 8 6 5 2

Dealer West,
Neither Vul.

10.
♠ A 9 5
♡ A K J
◇ J 6 5 2
♣ K 8 3

Dealer North,
Both Vul.

11.
♠ J 6 3
♡ J 8 4
◇ 2
♣ 10 9 8 7 5 3

Dealer East,
N-S Vul.

East opens 3♠, West bids 4♠.

12.
♠ K 10 8 6 3
♡ 7
◇ K 6
♣ Q 7 5 4 2

Dealer East,
N-S Vul.

East opens 2♡.

13.
♠ A 8
♡ K 10 9 8
◇ 8 7
♣ A 9 8 6 5

Dealer North,
Neither Vul.

14.
♠ Q J 9 3
♡ K Q 8 5
◇ A 9 3
♣ 5 2

Dealer South,
E-W Vul.

15.
♠ A 9 7 4 2
♡ A 7
◇ J 7 6 5 2
♣ 9

Dealer East,
Neither Vul.

16.
♠ Q 9 6 2
♡ K Q J 10 4 2
◇ A K 8
♣ —

Dealer North,
E-W Vul.

17.
♠ K J
♡ Q 9 7 5 3
◇ A Q 10 7
♣ A J

Dealer West,
N-S Vul.

West opens 3◇

18.
♠ —
♡ A 9 5
◇ K Q 5 4 3
♣ J 10 8 6 2

Dealer West,
Neither Vul.

East bids spades, West raises to 3♠ if possible; if it's a jump, it's weak.

19.
♠ A 2
♡ Q 4 3
◇ A 10 9
♣ A K 8 5 4

Dealer East,
N-S Vul.

East opens 3♠, West bids 4♠.

20.
♠ A K J 9 2
♡ K Q
◇ Q 3 2
♣ J 4 3

Dealer West,
Both Vul.

East bids 2◇; if North opens 1NT, the 2◇ bid shows diamonds and a major; if this is doubled by South, it goes redouble for rescue (by West), pass, pass.

1. ♠ A 8 3   *Dealer East,*
♡ K 7 5   *N-S Vul.*
◇ Q 6
♣ A Q J 9 3

2. ♠ A J 10 4 3   *Dealer South,*
♡ 2   *N-S Vul.*
◇ 7
♣ J 9 6 5 4 2

3. ♠ Q 10 9 5 3   *Dealer East,*
♡ 7 5 3   *N-S Vul.*
◇ K 6 4 3
♣ 7

East opens 1♡, West bids clubs and East bids 5♣.

4. ♠ K Q 8 5   *Dealer West,*
♡ A Q 9 7   *Both Vul.*
◇ 6
♣ Q 9 4 2

East bids spades and West raises if below 4♠ level.

5. ♠ K 7   *Dealer North,*
♡ K J 7   *Both Vul.*
◇ Q J 7 5
♣ J 6 4 2

East opens 1♣ (if possible), West responds 1♠, and East bids 2♠.

6. ♠ K 8   *Dealer South,*
♡ J   *Both Vul.*
◇ A J 9 7 4
♣ K 9 7 6 3

7. ♠ A J 3 2   *Dealer West,*
♡ K 10   *Neither Vul.*
◇ 8 7 6 2
♣ 9 5 3

8. ♠ —   *Dealer West,*
♡ 5 3   *N-S Vul.*
◇ K J 4 3
♣ A J 10 9 8 5 2

West opens 3♠, East bids 4♠ if possible.

9. ♠ A 8   *Dealer West,*
♡ Q 6 4 3   *E-W Vul.*
◇ Q 6 3 2
♣ A 7 3

10. ♠ A 2   *Dealer North,*
♡ A K J 8 7 3 2   *E-W Vul.*
◇ A 10 7
♣ J

11. ♠ A 8 7 4   *Dealer South,*
♡ A Q 3   *E-W Vul.*
◇ 9 4
♣ A J 8 6

12. ♠ K Q 9 5 4 2   *Dealer North,*
♡ —   *Neither Vul.*
◇ J 10 8
♣ A Q 9 2

13. ♠ Q 7 6 2   *Dealer East,*
♡ A Q J 9 6 5 3   *N-S Vul.*
◇ 10
♣ J

14. ♠ J 9 4 2   *Dealer South,*
♡ K J   *N-S Vul.*
◇ A 3
♣ A K 10 9 6

15. ♠ K 10 9 2   *Dealer East,*
♡ 9   *N-S Vul.*
◇ J 5 3
♣ A K Q 9 6

West bids 2♠.

16. ♠ A 6 5 2   *Dealer North,*
♡ 6 4   *Both Vul.*
◇ A 9 5 2
♣ J 10 9

East bids diamonds, West bids minimum number of spades (not forcing).

17. ♠ A J 9 3   *Dealer East,*
♡ A Q 3 2   *E-W Vul.*
◇ Q 9
♣ 8 3 2

18. ♠ A 10 8 6   *Dealer East,*
♡ Q 5 2   *Both Vul.*
◇ 8 4 3
♣ 10 8 2

West bids 1♡ if possible.

19. ♠ 7   *Dealer East,*
♡ K Q 10 8 7 6 5   *Neither Vul.*
◇ 8 7
♣ Q J 2

West	North	East	South
		pass	1♠
3♡	3NT	4♡	4NT
pass	6◇	pass	6NT
pass	pass	dbl	7♠
all pass			

What is your opening lead as West?

20. ♠ A Q 5   *Dealer South,*
♡ J 5   *N-S Vul.*
◇ 10 8 5 3
♣ K 6 4 3

West	North	East	South
			3♠
pass	4♠	dbl	all pass

What is your opening lead as West?

1.
♠ K Q 8 7
♡ K J 6 5
◇ 7 2
♣ K Q 4

Dealer North,
N-S Vul.

North opens 1♠. South bids 1NT if possible,
North bids 2◇ if possible and South raises to
3◇ if possible.

2.
♠ K 10 8 2
♡ J 3
◇ Q J 8 7
♣ J 7 3

Dealer East,
E-W Vul.

South opens 1♣.

3.
♠ A K Q 3
♡ J 8 5 3 2
◇ Q 9 5
♣ K

Dealer East,
N-S Vul.

South bids 1♠.

4.
♠ K J 7 6 3
♡ A Q 7 5
◇ 5
♣ Q J 6

Dealer East,
Both Vul.

5.
♠ A 10
♡ A Q 9 5 3
◇ K J 9 6 5
♣ K

Dealer North,
Both Vul.

6.
♠ 9
♡ A Q 9 6
◇ J 8 7 6
♣ Q 9 8 3

Dealer East,
Neither Vul.

7.
♠ 7
♡ K Q J 6 4 3
◇ J 7 5 3
♣ K Q

Dealer East,
E-W Vul.

8.
♠ A 9 7 6
♡ K 5 4 3
◇ 6 4
♣ A 6 3

Dealer North,
E-W Vul.

North opens 3♡.

9.
♠ Q 9 5
♡ K J
◇ 8 6 5 4
♣ K Q 9 3

Dealer East,
Both Vul.

10.
♠ J 10
♡ A 2
◇ K 9 4
♣ A 10 9 7 6 5

Dealer South,
N-S Vul.

South opens 2♡ and North bids 3♡.

11.
♠ K Q 5 2
♡ Q
◇ K J 2
♣ K 8 7 6 3

Dealer West,
Both Vul.

North bids 2◇.

12.
♠ J 2
♡ A K J 10 9 8 7 5 4
◇ A
♣ 3

Dealer North,
E-W Vul.

13.
♠ 8 2
♡ A
◇ 3 2
♣ A K Q 8 7 5 4 2

Dealer North,
E-W Vul.

North opens 2♠.

14.
♠ J 6 5 4
♡ A K 10 6
◇ Q 6
♣ A 4 2

Dealer East,
Both Vul.

15.
♠ Q J 6 5
♡ Q J 10 5
◇ Q 10 9
♣ 9 8

Dealer North,
Both Vul.

16.
♠ J 7 6 5
♡ K 8 4 2
◇ A
♣ A K 7 6

Dealer South,
Neither Vul.

South opens 4◇ showing a good 4♠ opening,
North bids 4♠ if possible.

17.
♠ K 6
♡ K 10 9 5
◇ Q 8 7
♣ A 8 4 2

Dealer East,
Neither Vul.

18.
♠ A K Q 7
♡ 8 4
◇ 2
♣ K J 8 7 4 2

Dealer North,
N-S Vul.

19.
♠ 2
♡ A K J 9 5
◇ K 4 3
♣ 8 7 5 3

Dealer West,
Both Vul.

20.
♠ 10 5
♡ A 9 4
◇ A K J 7 6 2
♣ 8 6

Dealer East,
Both Vul.

HANDS TO BID

1.
♠ K J 8 7
♡ A Q 4
◇ A 10 6
♣ Q 10 3

Dealer South,
E-W Vul.

South passes, but later enters with a diamond bid at any level.

2.
♠ K J 10
♡ A 10 6 5
◇ A K 9 7 3
♣ A

Dealer West,
Both Vul.

3.
♠ —
♡ J 7 5 3
◇ K J 9 6
♣ Q 10 6 3 2

Dealer East,
N-S Vul.

4.
♠ J 8
♡ A 10 9 8 4
◇ A K Q 8 7
♣ 10

Dealer North,
E-W Vul.

5.
♠ A J 7 5 4
♡ 8 6 4
◇ A J 4
♣ J 6

Dealer West,
Neither Vul.

6.
♠ 6 5 2
♡ 10 9 7 5 3
◇ A 7 5
♣ A Q

Dealer North,
E-W Vul.

7.
♠ K 5
♡ K Q J 6
◇ K 9 6 2
♣ 9 6 4

Dealer South,
E-W Vul.

8.
♠ 9 4 2
♡ 9
◇ K Q J 9 3 2
♣ 10 9 4

Dealer West,
Neither Vul.

9.
♠ K
♡ A Q 9
◇ A Q 9 8 5
♣ Q 10 7 4

Dealer North,
E-W Vul.

10.
♠ A Q 10 2
♡ J 4
◇ K 5 4 3
♣ K J 3

Dealer East,
Both Vul.

South overcalls in hearts, and North jump-raises hearts, skipping a level.

11.
♠ K
♡ A 8 6
◇ J 8 7 6 5 4
♣ A K 3

Dealer North,
Neither Vul.

South bids hearts and North raises one level.

12.
♠ Q 5
♡ —
◇ A Q 9 8 5 4 2
♣ A K J 3

Dealer South,
Both Vul.

13.
♠ A 10 9 7 2
♡ —
◇ K J 10 6 4 3 2
♣ 7

Dealer South,
Neither Vul.

South opens 3♡.

14.
♠ K 6 4 2
♡ A 7
◇ A 7 6
♣ K Q 8 4

Dealer North,
Both Vul.

15.
♠ K Q 8 4 3
♡ 7 4 2
◇ A Q
♣ K 7 5

Dealer North,
Neither Vul.

North opens 2♡.

16.
♠ 5
♡ A 8 5 3
◇ 3
♣ A K J 7 6 5 2

Dealer East,
E-W Vul.

17.
♠ A Q J 7 5 3
♡ —
◇ 8 6 5 4
♣ 7 6 4

Dealer East,
Neither Vul.

South overcalls in hearts and North raises one level.

18.
♠ A 8 6 3
♡ Q 10 5
◇ K 9 4
♣ 9 7 4

Dealer North,
Both Vul.

19.
♠ A Q 6
♡ 5 3
◇ A
♣ A K 10 9 8 7 4

Dealer South,
N-S Vul.

North overcalls in hearts.

20.
♠ K Q 6
♡ A J 8
◇ K 10 3
♣ J 10 8 7

Dealer West,
Both Vul.

1. ♠ K 8 7   *Dealer West,*
♡ A K Q 9 8 6 4   *Both Vul.*
◇ 4
♣ A J

South bids diamonds.

2. ♠ 4   *Dealer West,*
♡ K 10 7   *N-S Vul.*
◇ 9 8 5 4
♣ A K 7 6 3

3. ♠ A 9 8 4 2   *Dealer East,*
♡ J 5   *Both Vul.*
◇ A 2
♣ J 8 6 4

4. ♠ A K 4 3   *Dealer West,*
♡ A 10 9 8 5   *N-S Vul.*
◇ Q 5
♣ K 10

5. ♠ J 10   *Dealer North,*
♡ 6 3   *Both Vul.*
◇ K J 10 7 6 4 3 2
♣ 2

*South bids spades, North bids 3♠ and South
bids 4♠.*

6. ♠ A 6   *Dealer South,*
♡ J 8 5 3   *Both Vul.*
◇ A K Q 10 8 6
♣ 8

7. ♠ J 5 4   *Dealer West,*
♡ 8 6 3 2   *E-W Vul.*
◇ A 3
♣ K Q J 3

South bids 2♡, North bids 4♡.

8. ♠ 8 5 3   *Dealer South,*
♡ A K J 10 9 2   *Both Vul.*
◇ 7
♣ K J 5

South opens 1◇.

9. ♠ 7   *Dealer South,*
♡ A J 10 9   *Neither Vul.*
◇ K 9 6 3 2
♣ K 9 8

South passes, then bids spades. North bids 4♠.

10. ♠ J 4 2   *Dealer West,*
♡ —   *Neither Vul.*
◇ A K Q 9 8 6 4
♣ Q J 5

11. ♠ 7 6   *Dealer West,*
♡ A K   *N-S Vul.*
◇ A K Q 9 5
♣ A J 10 3

12. ♠ 7 6   *Dealer East,*
♡ K 10 9 5 3   *N-S Vul.*
◇ A 10 9 8 6 4
♣ —

13. ♠ 9 8 3   *Dealer West,*
♡ 3   *Both Vul.*
◇ 5 3 2
♣ A Q 10 9 7 3

14. ♠ K 10 7 6   *Dealer North,*
♡ A 9 2   *Both Vul.*
◇ A K 10 9 2
♣ 4

15. ♠ A J 10 7   *Dealer North,*
♡ K Q 10 7 4 2   *Neither Vul.*
◇ 10
♣ A 6

1. ♠ J 10 7 5 4   *Dealer West,*
    ♡ A Q   *Both Vul.*
    ♢ 10
    ♣ A K 5 4 3

2. ♠ A Q J 5   *Dealer West,*
    ♡ A 6   *Both Vul.*
    ♢ A 4 3
    ♣ Q 6 4 3

3. ♠ J 9 7   *Dealer East,*
    ♡ A   *E-W Vul.*
    ♢ A K 9 8 6
    ♣ A 10 8 7

West bids spades at the minimum level.

4. ♠ K 10 3   *Dealer East,*
    ♡ A 6   *E-W Vul.*
    ♢ A J 10 5 3 2
    ♣ Q 10

5. ♠ 9 6 4   *Dealer South,*
    ♡ A K   *N-S Vul.*
    ♢ K 6 4
    ♣ A 7 5 3 2

6. ♠ K 10   *Dealer North,*
    ♡ K 9 6 4 2   *Both Vul.*
    ♢ K 6 4 3
    ♣ 6 3

7. ♠ Q 10 8 4   *Dealer West,*
    ♡ 9 3   *Both Vul.*
    ♢ K 10 9
    ♣ J 10 9 7

East bids spades at the minimum level.

8. ♠ Q 7 6 3   *Dealer North,*
    ♡ 9   *Neither Vul.*
    ♢ K J 6 5 4 2
    ♣ A J

9. ♠ J 10 4   *Dealer North,*
    ♡ Q J 10   *E-W Vul.*
    ♢ A Q 10 9 7 5
    ♣ 10

10. ♠ A K 8 3 2   *Dealer East,*
    ♡ 2   *Both Vul.*
    ♢ J 10 5 4
    ♣ A 5 3

11. ♠ A Q J 10 4 2   *Dealer East,*
    ♡ 4   *Neither Vul.*
    ♢ Q 4
    ♣ A K J 6

12. ♠ K 6   *Dealer East,*
    ♡ K Q   *E-W Vul.*
    ♢ A J 9 8 5 4
    ♣ 8 5 3

13. ♠ K 10 9 5   *Dealer South,*
    ♡ —   *Both Vul.*
    ♢ 10 9 6 4 3
    ♣ K J 8 2

West bids hearts at the minimum level and East single jump-raises hearts.

14. ♠ K 10 9   *Dealer East,*
    ♡ 9 8 7   *E-W Vul.*
    ♢ 7 4
    ♣ A 9 7 4 3

East deals and opens 1♢, West passes.

15. ♠ A 7   *Dealer North,*
    ♡ A J 8 3   *E-W Vul.*
    ♢ K 10
    ♣ Q J 7 6 4

16. ♠ 7 2   *Dealer East,*
    ♡ J 7 6   *N-S Vul.*
    ♢ A Q
    ♣ K Q J 7 3 2

17. ♠ J 8 7 6 4 2   *Dealer North,*
    ♡ A Q 7 6   *Neither Vul.*
    ♢ —
    ♣ Q 8 2

18. ♠ A 5 4 3   *Dealer South,*
    ♡ 9   *Neither Vul.*
    ♢ A K Q 2
    ♣ Q J 7 6

West cuebids if possible to show majors, and East bids 2♡ if possible at his first turn.

19. ♠ 8 4 2   *Dealer South,*
    ♡ A 9   *Both Vul.*
    ♢ A K Q 8 7 6 4
    ♣ 8

20. ♠ A 10   *Dealer West,*
    ♡ K 10 8 4   *N-S Vul.*
    ♢ K 9 8 6 5 2
    ♣ 7

1.
♠ J 10 8 4
♡ A 9 3
◇ 7
♣ A K J 8 4

Dealer West,
N-S Vul.

West opens 2◇, East bids 3◇.

2.
♠ A J 3
♡ Q 8 7 3
◇ K 5 4
♣ Q 6 5

Dealer South,
Neither Vul.

3.
♠ A 10 8 5 2
♡ —
◇ A K 10 5
♣ A Q 9 5

Dealer South,
N-S Vul.

East overcalls 1♡ if possible, after which West jump-raises hearts.

4.
♠ K 10
♡ A K J
◇ A J 6
♣ K Q J 9 6

Dealer North,
E-W Vul.

5.
♠ A Q 10 6 3
♡ K 5 3
◇ A
♣ A Q 10 6

Dealer East,
N-S Vul.

6.
♠ K 5 4 2
♡ 10
◇ K Q 7 2
♣ A J 8 6

Dealer South,
N-S Vul.

West bids 1♠ if possible.

7.
♠ J 9 5
♡ J 6
◇ A K 7 3
♣ K 10 7 6

Dealer East,
N-S Vul.

8.
♠ A K 7 6
♡ K Q 8 6 5 3
◇ 8
♣ J 5

Dealer West,
Both Vul.

9.
♠ 10
♡ A K 10 5
◇ A K 8 6 5
♣ K Q 4

Dealer East,
E-W Vul.

10.
♠ 4
♡ J 8 2
◇ Q 7 5 3
♣ K J 9 7 4

Dealer East,
Both Vul.

11.
♠ A J
♡ A Q 10 6
◇ A J 6 4
♣ K 10 3

Dealer North,
Neither Vul.

12
♠ A J 7 2
♡ K 10 7 6 5
◇ J 4
♣ A 10

Dealer South,
E-W Vul.

13.
♠ K Q
♡ K 10 6 5
◇ K 2
♣ A K Q 10 2

Dealer East,
Both Vul.

14.
♠ K J 8
♡ A K J 9
◇ Q 10 9 2
♣ 10 5

Dealer West,
N-S Vul.

15.
♠ —
♡ K 8 5 2
◇ A 9 8 7 6 4 3
♣ 6 4

Dealer South,
Neither Vul.

East bids 2♠, West raises spades one level.

16.
♠ K Q 4 3
♡ J 7 5 3
◇ K 7
♣ Q 8 3

Dealer North,
Neither Vul.

17.
♠ A K J 9
♡ A J 10 7 4
◇ K Q 4
♣ Q

Dealer North,
Both Vul.

If possible, East opens 2♣ (natural, 11-15). West raises to 3♣.

18.
♠ J 9 6 5
♡ A 9 8 5
◇ J 5 4 3 2
♣ —

Dealer South,
N-S Vul.

West opens 1♣.

19.
♠ K Q 8 2
♡ A 10 7 4
◇ K J 9 3
♣ 8

Dealer South,
Both Vul.

20.
♠ Q 6 4
♡ K Q 2
◇ A 9
♣ K Q J 8 2

Dealer East,
Both Vul.

East opens 3◇.

1. ♠ 9 3   *Dealer West,*
       ♡ K 8   *Both Vul.*
       ◊ A K Q J 4
       ♣ A Q J 8

East bids 1♠.

2. ♠ 8 4 2   *Dealer East,*
       ♡ Q J 8 7 6 4 *Both Vul.*
       ◊ 6 5 2
       ♣ J

3. ♠ K J 9 5   *Dealer East,*
       ♡ Q 7 5 3   *N-S Vul.*
       ◊ K 8 5
       ♣ A 5

West bids 1♡ if possible, and East raises hearts one level.

4. ♠ A 8 6 5   *Dealer West,*
       ♡ 2   *Both Vul.*
       ◊ A K 7 5 4 2
       ♣ 6 5

West opens 2♡ (0-11 HCP, at least nine cards in the majors, 5-4 either way); East passes.

5. ♠ 7   *Dealer West,*
       ♡ K Q 10 9 7 5 2 *N-S Vul.*
       ◊ 10
       ♣ A 10 5 3

East overcalls 1♠ if possible, and, if he does, West raises to 5♠!

6. ♠ A 9 8   *Dealer West,*
       ♡ A 10 7   *Both Vul.*
       ◊ —
       ♣ K Q J 6 4 3 2

7. ♠ 9 6 3   *Dealer East,*
       ♡ J 9 8 2   *Both Vul.*
       ◊ K 2
       ♣ A K Q 2

East opens 1◊, West raises to 2◊.

8. ♠ Q 10 4   *Dealer East,*
       ♡ Q 9 5   *Both Vul.*
       ◊ A Q
       ♣ A K J 8 3

9. ♠ K J 9   *Dealer West,*
       ♡ A Q 9 8 4 *Neither Vul.*
       ◊ K 4
       ♣ K Q 4

10. ♠ K Q J 8 6 4 *Dealer North,*
       ♡ Q 4 2   *Both Vul.*
       ◊ K Q 8 3
       ♣ —

11. ♠ 4   *Dealer East,*
       ♡ A K Q 7 6 3 *N-S Vul.*
       ◊ 10 7 6
       ♣ A K Q

East opens 3♠, West bids 4♠.

12. ♠ Q J   *Dealer East,*
       ♡ K 6 2   *N-S Vul.*
       ◊ A Q 10 8 5 2
       ♣ K 9

East opens 2♡.

13. ♠ K 10 3 2   *Dealer North,*
       ♡ —   *Neither Vul.*
       ◊ A K 9 4 2
       ♣ K Q J 2

14. ♠ 4 2   *Dealer South,*
       ♡ A J 10 9 7 *E-W Vul.*
       ◊ J 6
       ♣ K Q 7 6

15. ♠ K 6 5   *Dealer East,*
       ♡ J 10 3   *Neither Vul.*
       ◊ A
       ♣ A K Q J 6 4

16. ♠ A J 10   *Dealer North,*
       ♡ 9 6   *E-W Vul.*
       ◊ 7 4 3 2
       ♣ Q 5 4 2

17. ♠ A Q 7 5 3 2 *Dealer West,*
       ♡ A 8   *N-S Vul.*
       ◊ 4
       ♣ K 10 8 5

West opens 3◊.

18. ♠ A 10 3   *Dealer West,*
       ♡ K 6 4   *Neither Vul.*
       ◊ J 10 9 2
       ♣ K Q 5

East bids spades, West raises to 3♠ if possible; if it's a jump, it's weak.

19. ♠ 4   *Dealer East,*
       ♡ A 6 5 2   *N-S Vul.*
       ◊ J 8 7 6 4
       ♣ Q 10 9

East opens 3♠, West bids 4♠.

20. ♠ Q 10 7 5   *Dealer West,*
       ♡ J 9 2   *Both Vul.*
       ◊ K 6 5
       ♣ K 9 6

East bids 2◊; if North opens 1NT, 2◊ = ◊ + a major. If South doubles, it goes redouble (rescue), pass, pass.

1
♠ K 9 7
♡ A J 9 8 2
◊ K 7 3 2
♣ 7

Dealer East,
N-S Vul.

2.
♠ K 6
♡ A K 9 8 4
◊ A J 10
♣ A K 8

Dealer South,
N-S Vul.

3.
♠ A K 4
♡ A 10 9
◊ A Q J 7 5
♣ 6 5

Dealer East,
N-S Vul.

East opens 1♡, West bids clubs and East bids 5♣.

4.
♠ 6
♡ 4
◊ 8 7 5 3 2
♣ A K J 8 5 3

Dealer West,
Both Vul.

East bids spades and West raises if below 4♠ level.

5.
♠ A 8
♡ 10 9 8
◊ A K 10 2
♣ K 8 5 3

Dealer North,
Both Vul.

East opens 1♣ (if possible), West responds 1♠, and East bids 2♠

6.
♠ A Q 5 4
♡ 5 4 3
◊ K Q 10
♣ Q 8 5

Dealer South,
Both Vul.

7.
♠ K Q 10 9 7
♡ A 9 7 6
◊ A
♣ 7 6 4

Dealer West,
Neither Vul.

8.
♠ 10 2
♡ A K J 8 2
◊ A 10 8 6 5
♣ 3

Dealer West,
N-S Vul.

West opens 3♠, East bids 4♠ if possible.

9.
♠ Q 3
♡ A K J 7 5 2
◊ A 10 9 7
♣ 9

Dealer West,
E-W Vul.

10.
♠ Q 4
♡ Q 6
◊ J 6 5 4 3 2
♣ A K 4

Dealer North,
E-W Vul.

11.
♠ K 6 5 3
♡ K J 9
◊ A Q J 10 8
♣ 5

Dealer South,
E-W Vul.

12.
♠ A 6
♡ K Q 9 6 3
◊ A K 6
♣ 10 8 7

Dealer North,
Neither Vul.

13.
♠ 4
♡ K 8 4
◊ A 9 8 2
♣ A Q 8 6 4

Dealer East,
N-S Vul.

14.
♠ A K
♡ A Q 9 7 4 2
◊ Q J 5
♣ Q J

Dealer South,
N-S Vul.

15.
♠ A Q 4
♡ A K Q J 6 5
◊ A 8
♣ 8 5

Dealer East,
N-S Vul.

West bids 2♠.

16.
♠ 4
♡ K Q 10 8
◊ 7
♣ A Q 8 7 6 5 3

Dealer North,
Both Vul.

East bids diamonds, West bids minimum number of spades (not forcing).

17.
♠ Q 8 7
♡ J 8 6
◊ 8 5
♣ A K J 10 6

Dealer East,
E-W Vul.

18.
♠ 9 7 3
♡ A 4
◊ A K 7
♣ A Q J 7 6

Dealer East,
Both Vul.

West bids 1♡ if possible

19.
♠ 7
♡ K Q 10 8 7 6 5
◊ 8 7
♣ Q J 2

Dealer East,
Neither Vul.

West	North	East	South
		pass	1♠
3♡	3NT	4♡	4NT
pass	6◊	pass	6NT
pass	pass	dbl	7♠
all pass			

What is your opening lead as West?

20.
♠ A Q 5
♡ J 5
◊ 10 8 5 3
♣ K 6 4 3

Dealer South,
N-S Vul.

West	North	East	South
			3♠
pass	4♠	dbl	all pass

What is your opening lead as West?

1. ♠ 9 3 *Dealer North,*
♡ A 7 2 *N-S Vul.*
◇ 4
♣ A 10 8 6 5 3 2

North opens 1♠. South bids 1NT if possible,
North bids 2◇ if possible and South raises to
3◇ if possible.

2. ♠ A Q J *Dealer East,*
♡ K Q 9 7 5 2 *E-W Vul.*
◇ A 9 6
♣ 10

South opens 1♣.

3. ♠ J 4 *Dealer East,*
♡ K 7 4 *N-S Vul.*
◇ A 8 4 2
♣ Q J 10 4

South bids 1♠.

4. ♠ A Q 2 *Dealer East,*
♡ J 9 6 3 *Both Vul.*
◇ K Q 10
♣ A 9 4

5. ♠ Q 9 2 *Dealer North,*
♡ J 7 *Both Vul.*
◇ A 3
♣ A Q J 10 3 2

6. ♠ A J 6 4 3 2 *Dealer East,*
♡ 8 3 *Neither Vul.*
◇ A K Q 2
♣ A

7. ♠ A Q J 10 *Dealer East,*
♡ A 5 *E-W Vul.*
◇ 10 9 2
♣ J 9 3 2

8. ♠ K J 4 3 *Dealer North,*
♡ 8 *E-W Vul.*
◇ A J 8 2
♣ 8 7 4 2

North opens 3♡.

9. ♠ K 8 3 *Dealer East,*
♡ A Q 7 6 4 3 *Both Vul.*
◇ A 7 3
♣ 5

10. ♠ A 6 5 2 *Dealer South,*
♡ 4 *N-S Vul.*
◇ A J 10 7 6 5
♣ K Q

South opens 2♡ and North bids 3♡.

11. ♠ 8 6 4 3 *West dealer,*
♡ A J 5 4 2 *Both Vul.*
◇ 4
♣ A Q J

North bids 2◇.

12. ♠ A 10 3 *Dealer North,*
♡ Q 3 2 *E-W Vul.*
◇ K J 8 7 6
♣ A K

13. ♠ J 10 *Dealer North,*
♡ Q 10 9 8 5 *E-W Vul.*
◇ A Q 9 5 4
♣ 6

North opens 2♠.

14. ♠ — *Dealer East,*
♡ Q 9 8 *Both Vul.*
◇ K 10 9 8
♣ K Q J 10 7 3

15. ♠ A K 10 3 *Dealer North,*
♡ K *Both Vul.*
◇ A 7 3 2
♣ Q J 7 6

16. ♠ — *Dealer South,*
♡ A 10 6 *Neither Vul.*
◇ Q J 9 3
♣ Q J 9 8 3 2

South opens 4◇ showing a good 4♠ opening;
North bids 4♠ if possible.

17. ♠ A 8 3 *Dealer East,*
♡ A 6 4 *Neither Vul.*
◇ A K J
♣ K 10 7 5

18. ♠ 10 3 2 *Dealer North,*
♡ A 7 5 3 *N-S Vul.*
◇ A Q 7
♣ A Q 5

19. ♠ A J 9 7 6 *Dealer West,*
♡ — *Both Vul.*
◇ Q
♣ K J 10 9 6 4 2

20. ♠ A K 7 6 4 3 2 *Dealer East,*
♡ K 2 *Both Vul.*
◇ Q 10
♣ A 9

1. ♠ Q   *Dealer South,*
     ♡ K J 6   *E-W Vul.*
     ◇ 7
     ♣ A K J 9 8 7 4 2
South passes, but later enters with a diamond bid at any level.

2. ♠ A 7 6 3   *Dealer West,*
     ♡ Q J 9 7 4 *Both Vul.*
     ◇ 8 4
     ♣ Q 8

3. ♠ A 8 5   *Dealer East,*
     ♡ A Q   *N-S Vul.*
     ◇ A 8 5 4 3 2
     ♣ A 7

4. ♠ A   *Dealer North,*
     ♡ K Q   *E-W Vul.*
     ◇ 10 4 3 2
     ♣ A J 9 8 7 3

5. ♠ K Q 6 3   *Dealer West,*
     ♡ K Q J 5   *Neither Vul.*
     ◇ K
     ♣ A 10 8 3

6. ♠ A Q J 3   *Dealer North,*
     ♡ K Q 2   *E-W Vul.*
     ◇ K 10 9
     ♣ 9 5 3

7. ♠ A 4 3   *Dealer South,*
     ♡ 2   *E-W Vul.*
     ◇ A 10 5 4
     ♣ A K J 7 3

8. ♠ A 8   *Dealer West,*
     ♡ A J 7 4 3 2 *Neither Vul.*
     ◇ 8 6
     ♣ A K Q

9. ♠ A Q 8 5 3 *Dealer North,*
     ♡ K 8   *E-W Vul.*
     ◇ J 7 6 4
     ♣ A K

10. ♠ K 8 6 5   *Dealer East,*
     ♡ —   *Both Vul.*
     ◇ A 8 2
     ♣ A Q 6 5 4 2
South overcalls in hearts, and North jump-raises hearts, skipping a level.

11. ♠ 10 9 5 3 2 *Dealer North,*
     ♡ 10 3   *Neither Vul.*
     ◇ A K Q 10 3
     ♣ 2
South bids hearts and North raises one level.

12. ♠ A K 9 7 2 *Dealer South,*
     ♡ K 8 3   *Both Vul.*
     ◇ 6
     ♣ Q 5 4 2

13. ♠ 3   *Dealer South,*
     ♡ K Q 9   *Neither Vul.*
     ◇ A Q 9
     ♣ A K Q J 6 4
South opens 3♡.

14. ♠ A Q J 5   *Dealer North,*
     ♡ K Q 10 8 4 3 *Both Vul.*
     ◇ 9
     ♣ A 6

15. ♠ A 10 2   *Dealer North,*
     ♡ A   *Neither Vul.*
     ◇ K 9 7 6 3
     ♣ A 9 6 3
North opens 2♡.

16. ♠ K Q J 10 9 3 *Dealer East,*
     ♡ 7 2   *E-W Vul.*
     ◇ K 6 4 2
     ♣ 8

17. ♠ K 10 9   *Dealer East,*
     ♡ 10 9 3   *Neither Vul.*
     ◇ A K J 7
     ♣ A J 3
South overcalls in hearts and North raises one level.

18. ♠ K Q 7 5   *Dealer North,*
     ♡ K 7 4 2   *Both Vul.*
     ◇ A Q 8
     ♣ K 3

19. ♠ K 9   *Dealer South,*
     ♡ J 4 2   *N-S Vul.*
     ◇ K 10 3 2
     ♣ Q J 6 3
North overcalls in hearts.

20. ♠ A 10 5 2   *Dealer West,*
     ♡ K 7   *Both Vul.*
     ◇ A Q 6
     ♣ A 6 5 3

1. ♠ Q J 10 2   *Dealer West,*
♡ 5 2   *Both Vul.*
◇ A K 9
♣ K 7 6 3

South bids diamonds

2. ♠ A 7   *Dealer West,*
♡ A Q J   *N-S Vul.*
◇ A K Q 10 7
♣ 10 4 2

3. ♠ K Q 6 3   *Dealer East,*
♡ A K 6   *Both Vul.*
◇ K 10 6 5
♣ K Q

4. ♠ Q 9 8 2   *Dealer West,*
♡ K 4 3   *N-S Vul.*
◇ A J
♣ A 8 6 3

5. ♠ A 7   *Dealer North,*
♡ A Q J 7 5   *Both Vul.*
◇ A 5
♣ A 8 6 3

*South bids spades, North bids 3♠ and South
bids 4♠.*

6. ♠ Q 9 8 5   *Dealer South,*
♡ A K   *Both Vul.*
◇ 7 5 4 3
♣ A 3 2

7. ♠ K Q 8 3   *Dealer West,*
♡ —   *E-W Vul.*
◇ K Q 10 9 8
♣ A 10 7 2

South bids 2♡, North bids 4♡.

8. ♠ A J 4   *Dealer South,*
♡ 7 6 4 3   *Both Vul.*
◇ K 8 5
♣ A 10 2

South opens 1◇.

9. ♠ 8 5 4   *Dealer South,*
♡ K Q   *Neither Vul.*
◇ A Q J 8 7
♣ A 5 3

South passes, then bids spades. North bids 4♠.

10. ♠ Q 6   *Dealer West,*
♡ A 9   *Neither Vul.*
◇ 7 5
♣ A K 10 9 8 4 3

11. ♠ Q   *Dealer West,*
♡ Q J 10 8 7 6 3 *N-S Vul.*
◇ 8 6 3
♣ Q 5

12. ♠ A K 2   *Dealer East,*
♡ Q J 8   *N-S Vul.*
◇ K 2
♣ A 9 6 4 3

13. ♠ A K 10   *Dealer West,*
♡ A 9 5   *Both Vul.*
◇ A K 9 8 4
♣ J 5

14. ♠ A 5   *Dealer North,*
♡ K J   *Both Vul.*
◇ Q J 7 5
♣ A J 10 8 3

15. ♠ Q 6 3   *Dealer North,*
♡ A   *Neither Vul.*
◇ A 8 6 5
♣ K Q 7 5 4

1.
♠ A
♡ 3
◊ A J 9 6 5 2
♣ Q 10 9 8 7
Dealer West,
Both Vul.

2.
♠ —
♡ K J 9 8 7 5
◊ K Q J 10 9 8
♣ J
Dealer West,
Both Vul.

3.
♠ A 10 5 2
♡ K 3
◊ Q J 10 7 2
♣ 6 4
Dealer East,
E-W Vul.

West bids spades at the minimum level.

4.
♠ A
♡ J 10 8 7 2
◊ K Q 6
♣ A J 5 3
Dealer East,
E-W Vul.

5.
♠ J 8
♡ Q 10 2
◊ A 10 9
♣ K Q J 9 8
Dealer South,
N-S Vul.

6.
♠ A 5 4
♡ A Q 5
◊ A J 7 2
♣ J 10 7
Dealer North,
Both Vul.

7.
♠ 9
♡ A Q J 7 6 5
◊ A 7 6
♣ K Q 8
Dealer West,
Both Vul.

East bids spades at the minimum level.

8.
♠ K
♡ A Q J 8 3
◊ A Q 9 3
♣ Q 7 4
Dealer North,
Neither Vul.

9.
♠ A 7 6
♡ A K
◊ —
♣ K Q J 8 7 6 5 4
Dealer North,
E-W Vul.

10.
♠ 10
♡ K 10 7
◊ A K 7 3 2
♣ K 10 7 6
Dealer East,
Both Vul.

11.
♠ 6
♡ A K 10 7 3
◊ A K 8 6 2
♣ 10 3
Dealer East,
Neither Vul.

12.
♠ A J 2
♡ J 9
◊ K 7
♣ A K Q J 9 7
Dealer East,
E-W Vul.

13.
♠ A 2
♡ Q 10 6 5
◊ A
♣ A 10 7 6 5 4
Dealer South,
Both Vul.

West bids hearts at the minimum level and
East single jump-raises hearts.

14.
♠ —
♡ K Q
◊ A K Q 5 2
♣ K Q J 8 6 5
Dealer East,
E-W Vul.

East deals and opens 1◊, West passes.

15.
♠ Q 6 4
♡ K
◊ A Q 9 7 5 4
♣ A 5 3
Dealer North,
E-W Vul.

16.
♠ 6 5 4 3
♡ A 8 3
◊ K 9 8 6 4
♣ A
Dealer East,
N-S Vul.

17.
♠ A K 9 5
♡ 10 9 3
◊ A K 5 4
♣ K J
Dealer North,
Neither Vul.

18.
♠ J
♡ A Q J 7
◊ J 9 8 4
♣ 10 8 4 2
Dealer South,
Neither Vul.

West cuebids if possible to show majors, and
East bids 2♡ if possible at his first turn.

19.
♠ 10 7 6
♡ K J 10 7
◊ J 2
♣ A K 6 5
Dealer South,
Both Vul.

20.
♠ K 9 7 6
♡ A Q J
◊ A 4 3
♣ Q 5 3
Dealer West,
N-S Vul.

1.   ♠ A K 9 2   *Dealer West,*
        ♡ K Q 6   *N-S Vul.*
        ◇ K 10 6
        ♣ 6 5 2

West opens 2◇, East bids 3◇.

2.   ♠ 10 9 8   *Dealer South,*
        ♡ A K J 6   *Neither Vul.*
        ◇ A Q 7
        ♣ A 3 2

3.   ♠ Q 9 7 4 3   *Dealer South,*
        ♡ 9 7 6 4 3   *N-S Vul.*
        ◇ Q 3
        ♣ 7

East overcalls 1♡ if possible, after which West jump-raises hearts.

4.   ♠ A Q 9 7 6   *Dealer North,*
        ♡ 7 3   *E-W Vul.*
        ◇ K 10 9 7
        ♣ 7 5

5.   ♠ K 9 8   *Dealer East,*
        ♡ A J 9 8 6   *N-S Vul.*
        ◇ 9 8 7
        ♣ K 7

6.   ♠ 7   *Dealer South,*
        ♡ A Q 9 6 4   *N-S Vul.*
        ◇ A 9
        ♣ K Q 9 7 5

West bids 1♠ if possible.

7.   ♠ K Q   *Dealer East,*
        ♡ A K 10 9 4 *N-S Vul.*
        ◇ Q
        ♣ A 9 8 4 3

8.   ♠ Q 4 3   *Dealer West,*
        ♡ A 9   *Both Vul.*
        ◇ A 7 4
        ♣ A Q 10 6 2

9.   ♠ A K 5 4   *Dealer East,*
        ♡ Q 8 7 6   *E-W Vul.*
        ◇ Q J 2
        ♣ 10 2

10. ♠ A K 5   *Dealer East,*
        ♡ A K 6   *Both Vul.*
        ◇ A 9 6 4
        ♣ 6 5 2

11. ♠ K Q 10   *Dealer North,*
        ♡ J 8 7 3   *Neither Vul.*
        ◇ 10 3 2
        ♣ A Q J

12. ♠ Q 10   *Dealer South,*
        ♡ 8 3 2   *E-W Vul.*
        ◇ A K Q 9 3 2
        ♣ Q 5

13. ♠ A 6 5   *Dealer East,*
        ♡ A 9 4 3   *Both Vul.*
        ◇ Q 10 7 5 3
        ♣ 3

14. ♠ A 9 6 5 4   *Dealer West,*
        ♡ 2   *N-S Vul.*
        ◇ A 4
        ♣ A K Q 9 3

15. ♠ 10 8 2   *Dealer South,*
        ♡ A   *Neither Vul.*
        ◇ Q J 5
        ♣ A Q 10 9 7 5

East bids 2♠, West raises spades one level.

16. ♠ A J 10 9 6 2 *Dealer North,*
        ♡ 8 2   *Neither Vul.*
        ◇ 6
        ♣ K J 7 4

17. ♠ Q 8 7   *Dealer North,*
        ♡ 9 8 5   *Both Vul.*
        ◇ A J 10 7 5
        ♣ 9 6

If possible, East opens 2♣ (natural, 11-15). West raises to 3♣.

18. ♠ 4 2   *Dealer South,*
        ♡ J 6 4   *N-S Vul.*
        ◇ K Q 10
        ♣ A K Q 8 6

West opens 1♣.

19. ♠ 9 4   *Dealer South,*
        ♡ K Q J 5 2   *Both Vul.*
        ◇ A 10 6
        ♣ K J 2

20. ♠ 10 9 2   *Dealer East,*
        ♡ A J 4 3   *Both Vul.*
        ◇ Q 3
        ♣ 10 9 7 6

East opens 3◇.

1. ♠ A J 2　　　*Dealer West,*
　　♡ 9 7 6 5　　*Both Vul.*
　　◇ 8
　　♣ 7 6 4 3 2

East bids 1♠.

2. ♠ A 5　　　*Dealer East,*
　　♡ A K　　　*Both Vul.*
　　◇ K Q 3
　　♣ A K 6 5 3 2

3. ♠ A 8 6 4 3 2　*Dealer East,*
　　♡ 10　　　　*N-S Vul.*
　　◇ Q 9
　　♣ 10 7 6 3

West bids 1♡ if possible, and East raises hearts one level.

4. ♠ J 2　　　*Dealer West,*
　　♡ A Q J 7 5　*Both Vul.*
　　◇ Q J 9 6
　　♣ 3 2

West opens 2♡ showing 0-11 HCP and at least nine cards in the majors, 5-4 either way; East passes.

5. ♠ Q 4　　　*Dealer West,*
　　♡ A 8 6 3　　*N-S Vul.*
　　◇ A Q 4 3
　　♣ K Q 9

East overcalls 1♠ if possible, and, if he does, West raises to 5♠!

6. ♠ Q J 10 7　*Dealer West,*
　　♡ Q 9 8 6 3　*Both Vul.*
　　◇ A Q 10 4
　　♣ —

7. ♠ A K Q　　*Dealer East,*
　　♡ 7 6　　　*Both Vul.*
　　◇ Q 5 4
　　♣ J 8 7 6 4

East opens 1◇, West raises 2◇.

8. ♠ K J 9 5　　*Dealer East,*
　　♡ A 8 6 3 2　*Both Vul.*
　　◇ 7
　　♣ Q 7 4

9. ♠ A Q 7　　*Dealer West,*
　　♡ 6 5 3　　*Neither Vul.*
　　◇ Q 7
　　♣ A 8 6 5 2

10. ♠ A 9 5　　*Dealer North,*
　　♡ A K J　　*Both Vul.*
　　◇ J 6 5 2
　　♣ K 8 3

11. ♠ J 6 3　　*Dealer East,*
　　♡ J 8 4　　*N-S Vul.*
　　◇ 2
　　♣ 10 9 8 7 5 3

East opens 3♠, West bids 4♠.

12. ♠ K 10 8 6 3　*Dealer East,*
　　♡ 7　　　　*N-S Vul.*
　　◇ K 6
　　♣ Q 7 5 4 2

East opens 2♡.

13. ♠ A 8　　　*Dealer North,*
　　♡ K 10 9 8　*Neither Vul.*
　　◇ 8 7
　　♣ A 9 8 6 5

14. ♠ Q J 9 3　*Dealer South,*
　　♡ K Q 8 5　*E-W Vul.*
　　◇ A 9 3
　　♣ 5 2

15. ♠ A 9 7 4 2　*Dealer East,*
　　♡ A 7　　　*Neither Vul.*
　　◇ J 7 6 5 2
　　♣ 9

16. ♠ Q 9 6 2　*Dealer North,*
　　♡ K Q J 10 4 2　*E-W Vul.*
　　◇ A K 8
　　♣ —

17. ♠ K J　　　*Dealer West,*
　　♡ Q 9 7 5 3　*N-S Vul.*
　　◇ A Q 10 7
　　♣ A J

West opens 3◇

18. ♠ —　　　*Dealer West,*
　　♡ A 9 5　　*Neither Vul.*
　　◇ K Q 5 4 3
　　♣ J 10 8 6 2

East bids spades, West raises to 3♠ if possible; if it's a jump, it's weak.

19. ♠ A 2　　　*Dealer East,*
　　♡ Q 4 3　　*N-S Vul.*
　　◇ A 10 9
　　♣ A K 8 5 4

East opens 3♠, West bids 4♠.

20. ♠ A K J 9 2　*Dealer West,*
　　♡ K Q　　　*Both Vul.*
　　◇ Q 3 2
　　♣ J 4 3

East bids 2◇; if North opens 1NT, the 2◇ bid shows diamonds and a major; if this is doubled by South, it goes redouble for rescue (by West), pass, pass.

1.
♠ A 8 3
♡ K 7 5
◇ Q 6
♣ A Q J 9 3

Dealer East,
N-S Vul.

2.
♠ A J 10 4 3
♡ 2
◇ 7
♣ J 9 6 5 4 2

Dealer South,
N-S Vul.

3.
♠ Q 10 9 5 3
♡ 7 5 3
◇ K 6 4 3
♣ 7

Dealer East,
N-S Vul.

East opens 1♡, West bids clubs and East bids 5♣.

4.
♠ K Q 8 5
♡ A Q 9 7
◇ 6
♣ Q 9 4 2

Dealer West,
Both Vul.

East bids spades and West raises if below 4♠ level.

5.
♠ K 7
♡ K J 7
◇ Q J 7 5
♣ J 6 4 2

Dealer North,
Both Vul.

East opens 1♣ (if possible), West responds 1♠, and East bids 2♠.

6.
♠ K 8
♡ J
◇ A J 9 7 4
♣ K 9 7 6 3

Dealer South,
Both Vul.

7.
♠ A J 3 2
♡ K 10
◇ 8 7 6 2
♣ 9 5 3

Dealer West,
Neither Vul.

8.
♠ —
♡ 5 3
◇ K J 4 3
♣ A J 10 9 8 5 2

Dealer West,
N-S Vul.

West opens 3♠, East bids 4♠ if possible.

9.
♠ A 8
♡ Q 6 4 3
◇ Q 6 3 2
♣ A 7 3

Dealer West,
E-W Vul.

10.
♠ A 2
♡ A K J 8 7 3 2
◇ A 10 7
♣ J

Dealer North,
E-W Vul.

11.
♠ A 8 7 4
♡ A Q 3
◇ 9 4
♣ A J 8 6

Dealer South,
E-W Vul.

12.
♠ K Q 9 5 4 2
♡ —
◇ J 10 8
♣ A Q 9 2

Dealer North,
Neither Vul.

13.
♠ Q 7 6 2
♡ A Q J 9 6 5 3
◇ 10
♣ J

Dealer East,
N-S Vul.

14.
♠ J 9 4 2
♡ K J
◇ A 3
♣ A K 10 9 6

Dealer South,
N-S Vul.

15.
♠ K 10 9 2
♡ 9
◇ J 5 3
♣ A K Q 9 6

Dealer East,
N-S Vul.

West bids 2♠.

16.
♠ A 6 5 2
♡ 6 4
◇ A 9 5 2
♣ J 10 9

Dealer North,
Both Vul.

East bids diamonds, West bids minimum number of spades (not forcing).

17.
♠ A J 9 3
♡ A Q 3 2
◇ Q 9
♣ 8 3 2

Dealer East,
E-W Vul.

18.
♠ A 10 8 6
♡ Q 5 2
◇ 8 4 3
♣ 10 8 2

Dealer East,
Both Vul.

West bids 1♡ if possible.

19.
♠ 7
♡ K Q 10 8 7 6 5
◇ 8 7
♣ Q J 2

Dealer East,
Neither Vul.

West	North	East	South
		pass	1♠
3♡	3NT	4♡	4NT
pass	6◇	pass	6NT
pass	pass	dbl	7♠
all pass			

What is your opening lead as West?

20.
♠ A Q 5
♡ J 5
◇ 10 8 5 3
♣ K 6 4 3

Dealer South,
N-S Vul.

West	North	East	South
			3♠
pass	4♠	dbl	all pass

What is your opening lead as West?

1.   ♠ K Q 8 7   *Dealer North,*
        ♡ K J 6 5   *N-S Vul.*
        ◇ 7 2
        ♣ K Q 4

North opens 1♠. South bids 1NT if possible,
North bids 2◇ if possible and South raises to
3◇ if possible.

2.   ♠ K 10 8 2   *Dealer East,*
        ♡ J 3   *E-W Vul.*
        ◇ Q J 8 7
        ♣ J 7 3

South opens 1♣.

3.   ♠ A K Q 3   *Dealer East,*
        ♡ J 8 5 3 2   *N-S Vul.*
        ◇ Q 9 5
        ♣ K

South bids 1♠.

4.   ♠ K J 7 6 3   *Dealer East,*
        ♡ A Q 7 5   *Both Vul.*
        ◇ 5
        ♣ Q J 6

5.   ♠ A 10   *Dealer North,*
        ♡ A Q 9 5 3   *Both Vul.*
        ◇ K J 9 6 5
        ♣ K

6.   ♠ 9   *Dealer East,*
        ♡ A Q 9 6   *Neither Vul.*
        ◇ J 8 7 6
        ♣ Q 9 8 3

7.   ♠ 7   *Dealer East,*
        ♡ K Q J 6 4 3 *E-W Vul.*
        ◇ J 7 5 3
        ♣ K Q

8.   ♠ A 9 7 6   *Dealer North,*
        ♡ K 5 4 3   *E-W Vul.*
        ◇ 6 4
        ♣ A 6 3

North opens 3♡.

9.   ♠ Q 9 5   *Dealer East,*
        ♡ K J   *Both Vul.*
        ◇ 8 6 5 4
        ♣ K Q 9 3

10. ♠ J 10   *Dealer South,*
        ♡ A 2   *N-S Vul.*
        ◇ K 9 4
        ♣ A 10 9 7 6 5

South opens 2♡ and North bids 3♡.

11. ♠ K Q 5 2   *Dealer West,*
        ♡ Q   *Both Vul.*
        ◇ K J 2
        ♣ K 8 7 6 3

North bids 2◇.

12. ♠ J 2   *Dealer North,*
        ♡ A K J 10 9 8 7 5 4   *E-W Vul.*
        ◇ A
        ♣ 3

13. ♠ 8 2   *Dealer North,*
        ♡ A   *E-W Vul.*
        ◇ 3 2
        ♣ A K Q 8 7 5 4 2

North opens 2♠.

14. ♠ J 6 5 4   *Dealer East,*
        ♡ A K 10 6   *Both Vul.*
        ◇ Q 6
        ♣ A 4 2

15. ♠ Q J 6 5   *Dealer North,*
        ♡ Q J 10 5   *Both Vul.*
        ◇ Q 10 9
        ♣ 9 8

16. ♠ J 7 6 5   *Dealer South,*
        ♡ K 8 4 2   *Neither Vul.*
        ◇ A
        ♣ A K 7 6

South opens 4◇ showing a good 4♠ opening,
North bids 4♠ if possible.

17. ♠ K 6   *Dealer East,*
        ♡ K 10 9 5   *Neither Vul.*
        ◇ Q 8 7
        ♣ A 8 4 2

18. ♠ A K Q 7   *Dealer North,*
        ♡ 8 4   *N-S Vul.*
        ◇ 2
        ♣ K J 8 7 4 2

19. ♠ 2   *Dealer West,*
        ♡ A K J 9 5   *Both Vul.*
        ◇ K 4 3
        ♣ 8 7 5 3

20. ♠ 10 5   *Dealer East,*
        ♡ A 9 4   *Both Vul.*
        ◇ A K J 7 6 2
        ♣ 8 6